THE

RANGERS
FOOTBALL
MISCELLANY

This book is dedicated to my wife, Janice, our two sons, Marc and Paul, my father and mother, Johnny & Rosaleen White, my brother David and my sisters, Donna, Michelle and Danielle.

A team has the unwavering support of its fans. I have the loyal and dedicated support of my family.

Yours in appreciation from a husband, a father, a son and a brother.

John

This edition published in 2006

Copyright © Carlton Books Limited 2006

Carlton Books Limited
20 Mortimer Street
London W1T 3JW

A CIP catalogue record for this book is available from the British Library

ISBN-13: 978-184442-158-9
ISBN-10: 1-84442-158-9

Editor: Martin Corteel
Project art editor: Darren Jordan
Production: Lisa French

Printed in Great Britain

THE
RANGERS
FOOTBALL
MISCELLANY

JOHN WHITE

WITH A FOREWORD BY **WILLIE HENDERSON**

CARLTON
BOOKS

❈ ACKNOWLEDGEMENTS ❈

Special thanks to the webmaster at www.wikipedia.org for providing such an informative database on most football clubs around the world that helped me verify data and also helped me obtain information on a number of subjects.

My thanks to David Ross and Forrest Robertson at www.scottishleague. net, which provides a comprehensive, and regularly updated, section on Scottish football.

And thanks also to Iain McKee, Duncan Cameron, Garry Lynch, John Millar, Kirsty Price and Alan Thomson for taking the time to check the entries in my book for accuracy.

Thanks also to Gary the webmaster at the East Enclosure website – www. ayeready.com – for allowing me to use some material from his website and for taking the time to proofread my work.

❈ FOREWORD ❈

As a lifelong Glasgow Rangers fan I was delighted when John asked me to write the foreword to his *Rangers Football Miscellany*.

Needless to say, standing at just 5ft 4 inches in my socks, I was affectionately nicknamed "Wee Willie" by the Rangers fans.

Having made my debut for Rangers when I was just 17 years old, I was further honoured to be capped by my country a year later. I will always be grateful to the legendary Rangers manager, Scot Symon, for having the faith in my ability. However, without doubt the greatest moment of my Ibrox career came during the 1963–64 season, when I was so proud to be a member of only the second Rangers team ever to clinch the Scottish Treble of League Championship, League Cup and FA Cup.

And so to John's book. Having played for the club from the early 1960s up to 1972, and working for the club today on match days entertaining the fans in the suites at Ibrox, I thought I knew all there was to know about Rangers Football Club. However, after reading John's book I realized just how much I didn't know. John's book is a magical trip through the history of Rangers from the moment in 1872 when four young men (Peter Campbell, William McBeath, Peter McNeil and his brother, Moses McNeil) all met up to form a football club despite having no money, no football kit and not even a ball, up to the present day and the world stars that grace Ibrox Stadium week in and week out.

Just flicking through the pages helped me rekindle many, many warm and wonderful memories of former team-mates, magnificent matches, European glory nights, Old Firm encounters, breathtaking goals and the one thing I will never forget above all others, the sound of the Ibrox crowd willing the team on to win: all of them glorious memories, indeed, that will live with me forever.

No matter what page you turn to in John's book you will learn an interesting fact, or see a piece of trivia that will startle you, or you will find yourself reading about an unusual occurrence in the history of the club, and all with a statistic or two included for good measure. This is most definitely a "must have" book for all Rangers fans out there. The way John has put the book together has made it so easy to read time and time again without ever becoming bored with it, and above all else the *Rangers Football Miscellany* is a thoroughly enjoyable trip down memory lane covering 134 years of an illustrious history.

Willie Henderson
May 2006

❊ LIST OF ABBREVIATIONS ❊

EC	European Cup
ECWC	European Cup-winners' Cup
FA	Football Association
FC	Fairs Cup
FIFA	Federation of International Football Associations
ICFC	Inter-cities Fairs Cup
P/W/D/L/F/A	Played/Won/Drawn/Lost/(Goals)For/(Goals)Against
SC	Scottish FA Cup
SFA	Scottish Football Associations
SLC	Scottish League Cup
SPL	Scottish Premier League
UCL	UEFA Champions League
UEFA	Union of European Football Associations

❋ INTRODUCTION ❋

Think of Rangers Football Club and immediately the words "history", "honour", "pride", "loyalty" and "success" spring to mind. However, it could have been all so different had it not been for four young men in 1872. Peter Campbell, William McBeath and the McNeil brothers, Moses and Peter, had no money, no football kit and no football but what they had was a dream, a dream to form a football club in Glasgow. And thus, in 1872, Rangers Football Club was formed from very humble beginnings and today they are worshipped by millions of fans across the four corners of the world.

Rangers has been steeped in history almost from its formation right up until the present day, with the famous "Aye Ready" motto instantly recognizable around the world. There have been many defining moments that have helped shape the history of the 'Gers and, in this book, I will take you on a magical journey that will, hopefully, rekindle many wonderful moments, provide you with some unusual statistics, fascinating trivia, intriguing facts and figures about managers and players, plus many Cup, League and European glory day memories. However, my one hope after you read this book is that it will leave you scratching your head at least once for you to say, "I didn't know that". If I can make you do that, then all the hours I spent compiling the book will have been worthwhile.

Many wonderful players have graced the famous blue shirt of Rangers throughout their illustrious history and I am very proud to say that one of them in particular, Willie Henderson, very kindly provided the foreword for my book. Wee Willie was a prodigious talent who did for football in Scotland during the 1960s what the Beatles did for pop music at the same time. Wee Willie was only 17 years old when he made his Rangers debut and, a year later, played for Scotland. A player with unbelievable pace, he could also cross a ball as accurately as any player to grace the game, and he bagged a few goals. I thank him for his kind words about my book.

So in closing, I hope *The Rangers Football Miscellany* will not only bring back memories of that famous night in Barcelona in 1972, when Willie Waddell's 'Gers lifted the European Cup-Winners' Cup but also glimpses of Doubles, Trebles and many classic Old Firm encounters. No doubt you will have your very own special memories from matches you have attended or seen but I hope my book will bring many more to your attention from the club's golden years.

John White
May 2006

❋ SIMPLY THE BEST ❋

Graeme Souness started his career as an apprentice at Tottenham Hotspur under the legendary Bill Nicholson, but the young Scot grew impatient at his lack of first-team opportunities. He is famously reported to have told the 1961 Double-winning manager Bill Nicholson that he was the best player at White Hart Lane and should be in the team. After making a solitary appearance for the London club, Souness moved to Middlesbrough in 1973.

❋ BLUE RECORD HOLDERS ❋

On 23 February 1901, Scotland beat Ireland 11–0 in a Home Championship match at Celtic Park in front of 15,000 fans. The win is Scotland's record victory of all time and Old Firm players shared all 11 goals. The Scotland team that lined up that day was as follows: George Chappell McWattie (Queen's Park), Nicol Smith (Rangers), Bernard Battles (Celtic), David Kennedy Russell (Celtic), George Anderson (Kilmarnock), John Tait Robertson (Rangers), John Campbell (Rangers), John Campbell (Celtic), Robert Cumming Hamilton (Rangers), Alexander McMahon (Celtic), Alexander Smith (Rangers).

❋ THE IBROX DISASTER ❋

On 2 January 1971, Celtic were on their way to securing their sixth successive Scottish League title, but still had to play Rangers at Ibrox. At the end of the Old Firm derby that fateful day, the steel barriers on stairway 13 gave way and a total of 66 people were suffocated to death, with dozens more injured in the resulting carnage. It was originally believed that after Colin Stein had scored a dramatic equalizer for Rangers in the final seconds of the game – just a minute after Jimmy Johnstone had put Celtic 1–0 up – fans who were on their way out of the stadium turned to come back in and ran head-first into a mass of jubilant fans coming in the opposite direction. However, the inquiry that followed this horrific disaster found that assumption to be completely wrong. What in fact happened was that the crowd remained to the end and, when they were exiting, a crush happened halfway down stairway 13[†].

'The game itself had been played in a very sporting manner and, out of a crowd of 80,000 fans, only two arrests had been made by the police, both of them for drunkenness. After the disaster, Rangers and Celtic came together to help the victims of the tragedy and a special match between Scotland and a Rangers/Celtic Select XI was played in front of an attendance of 81,405 at Hampden Park.

✳ RANGERS XI OF THE 1870s ✳

1
James
WATT

2
George
GILLESPIE

3
Tom
VALLANCE

4
Willie
McNEIL

5
Sam
RICKETTS

6
Willie
DUNLOP

7
David
HILL

8
James
WATSON

9
Alex
MARSHALL

10
Peter
CAMPBELL

11
Moses
McNEIL

Reserves
John *YUIL* • James *CAMPBELL* • Hugh *McINTYRE*,
William *STRUTHERS* • John *CAMPBELL*
Honorary Match Secretary
Peter *McNEIL*

Did You Know That?
In the 1878–79 season, Rangers won their first ever Glasgow Merchants Cup and went on to win the trophy another 31 times.

✳ WIT AND WISDOM OF THE BLUES (1) ✳

"I only ever have a drink when we win a trophy. That's why people think I'm an alcoholic."
Iain Ferguson

✳ FERGIE FAVOURS DAVIE IN HIS FIRST GAME ✳

On 16 October 1985, Alex Ferguson took charge of Scotland for the first time in a friendly against East Germany at Hampden Park[†]. Alex played just one Rangers player, Davie Cooper, in the game that ended 0–0.

[†] Two future Rangers managers, Graeme Souness (Sampdoria) and Alex McLeish (Aberdeen), and a future Celtic manager, Kenny Dalglish (Liverpool), also played in the game.

❀ UP FOR THE CUP (1) ❀

On their way to their first Scottish Cup final in 1877, Rangers beat Queen's Park Juniors 4–1 (h) in the first round, Towerhill 8–0 (a) in the second round, Mauchline 3–0 (a) in the fourth round and Lennox 3–0 (a) in the quarter-final to secure a meeting with Vale of Leven in the final at the West of Scotland Cricket Ground on 17 March 1877. The game ended 1–1, as did the replay, after extra time, on 7 April. The second replay was played at First Hampden Park and Rangers lost 3–2.

SCOTTISH FA CUP FINAL (SECOND REPLAY)
13 APRIL 1877, HAMPDEN PARK, GLASGOW
Vale of Leven (1) 3   v.   Rangers (0) 2
(Watson o.g., Baird, Paton)   (Campbell, W. McNeil)
Att. 8,000
Rangers: James Watt, George Gillespie, Tom Vallance, Willie McNeil, Sam Ricketts, Willie Dunlop, David Hill, James Watson, Alex Marshall, Peter Campbell, Moses McNeil.

Did You Know That?
Rangers received a bye in both the third round and in the semi-final, while the extra time played in the first replay is believed to have been the first instance of it being played in the history of the game.

❀ RANGERS ON TOUR – 1904 ❀

Vienna......First Vienna FC v. Glasgow Rangers........................2–7 *(w)*
Vienna......Boldklub 1893 Copenhagen v. Glasgow Rangers.....0–9 *(w)*
Vienna......Boldklub 1893 Copenhagen v. Glasgow Rangers.....3–5 *(w)*
Vienna......Wiener AC v. Glasgow Rangers...............................0–8 *(w)*
Prague......Prague XI v. Glasgow Rangers.................................1–6 *(w)*
Prague......Slavia Prague v. Glasgow Rangers............................0–5 *(w)*

❀ SOUNESS LIKES WHAT HE SEES ❀

On 23 April 1986, captain Graeme Souness scored a penalty for Scotland against England in the Stanley Rous Cup at Wembley. Scotland lost the match 2–1, with future Rangers legend Terry Butcher scoring England's first goal. Other future Blues in the England line-up that day were Trevor Francis, Gary Stevens and Ray Wilkins, all of whom, plus Butcher, were signed by Souness when he became manager at Ibrox.

❋ SHIRT SPONSORS ❋

Rangers first wore a logo on their shirt in the 1984–85 season, when they signed a sponsorship deal with the Glasgow-based double-glazing firm, C.R. Smith[†]. Rangers' shirt sponsors to date include: C.R. Smith (1984–87), McEwan's Lager (1987–99), Ntl (1999–2003) and Carling (2003–).

❋ FIVE BHOYS TURN BLUE ❋

On 11 March 1959, a Rangers/Celtic Select XI side played at Telford Park, Inverness, to commemorate the switching on of Caledonian FC's new floodlight system. However, at the time, SFA regulations required all competing players to be signed to a single Scottish League member club, so the five Celtic players that had been selected to play signed for Rangers and then re-signed for Celtic the following day. The Rangers/Celtic Select XI, who won the game 4–2 in front of 6,000 fans, played in a kit of white shirts with blue and red hoops and white shorts, was as follows: Beattie (Celtic), King (Rangers), Kennedy (Celtic), Crerand (Celtic), Paterson (Rangers), Millar (Rangers), Tully (Celtic), Baird (Rangers), Conway (Celtic), Queen (Rangers), Hubbard (Rangers). Scot Symon, the Rangers manager, managed the side.

❋ DANISH DELIGHT FOR STEIN ❋

On 16 October 1968, Rangers' Colin Stein made a winning start to his international career when Scotland beat Denmark 1–0 in a friendly at Idraetsparken, Copenhagen.

❋ BRAND TO THE RESCUE ❋

Following Scotland's 9–3 humiliation at the hands of England at Wembley on 15 April 1961, Scotland manager Ian McColl made six changes for Scotland's next game against Eire on 3 May 1961 in a World Cup qualifying group eight game. Not surprisingly, Celtic's shell-shocked goalkeeper, Frank Haffey, was dropped, but Rangers' Eric Caldow, who had captained the Scots against England, was retained, along with his Rangers team-mates Robert Shearer and Davie Wilson; Ibrox men Jim Baxter and Ralph Brand were both recalled to the side to win their second caps. Scotland won the game at Hampden Park 4–1, with Brand scoring twice.

[†]C.R. Smith also sponsored Celtic in the 1984–85 season.

❇ EVERY OTHER SATURDAY ❇

Every other Saturday's my half day off
And it's off to the match I go,
Happily we wander down the Paisley Road
Me and my wee pal Jock,
We love to see the lassies with their blue scarves on,
We love to hear the boys all roar,
But I don't have to tell you that the best of all,
We love to see the Rangers score,
Me oh me oh me oh my, Oh how we love to see them try,
We love to see the lassies with their blue scarves on,
We love to hear the boys all roar,
But I don't have to tell you that the best of all,
We love to see the Rangers score,
We've won the Scottish League about a thousand times
The Glasgow is as simple too,
We gave some exhibitions in the Scottish Cup,
We gave some Wembley wizards too,
And when the Rangers win the European Cup,
As we've done with the one before,
We'll gather round at Ibrox Park 100,000 strong,
And give the boys an Ibrox roar.

❇ INAUGURAL PREMIER DIVISION CHAMPIONS ❇

At the end of the 1974–75 season, the Scottish First Division was re-organized, with the teams finishing in the top ten positions of the old First Division forming the new Scottish Premier Division for the 1975–76 season. Rangers won the inaugural Scottish Premier Division in 1975–76.

❇ MILLAR'S SCOTLAND DEBUT ABANDONED ❇

On 8 May 1963, in what was supposed to be a friendly, Scotland's game against Austria had to be abandoned after 79 minutes because the referee, James Finney from England, felt that players risked serious injury if play was allowed to continue. Scotland were leading 4–1 at the time and the Austrians were already down to nine men, after Horst Nemec had been sent off for spitting and Erich Hof for a dangerous waist-high tackle. Davie Wilson and Denis Law had both scored twice for Scotland, while Rangers' young striker, James Millar, was making his international debut.

❋ RANGERS TIMELINE ❋

1873........ Rangers Football Club formed

1887........ Move from Burnbank to Kinnie Park

1890........ Rangers become a co-founder of the Scottish Football League

1891........ Win the first league title (although shared with Dumbarton)

1899........ Move to Ibrox Stadium

1899........ Win first outright league title and do not drop a single point

1901........ Become first Scottish club to win three consecutive league titles

1902........ Become first Scottish club to win four consecutive league titles

1926........ Win the Double for the first time

1930........ Create a world record by winning every competition they enter: Scottish League, Scottish FA Cup, Glasgow Cup, Glasgow Charity Cup, Second XI Cup and Reserve League Cup

1934........ Win the Double for the second time

1935........ Secure their third Double

1936........ Win the Scottish Cup for the third year in succession

1947........ Win 25th league championship and inaugural League Cup

1949........ Become first winners of Scottish Treble

1950........ Repeat feat of three consecutive Scottish Cup wins

1961........ Win the league championship for the 32nd time and the League Cup for the third time

1963........ Win the Double for the fifth time in the club's history

1964........ Win the Treble for the second time

1972........ Win the European Cup-Winners' Cup

1976........ Win the Treble for the third time

1978........ Win the Treble for the fourth time

1979........ Win the Scottish Cup for the 23rd time and the League Cup for the tenth time

1993........ Win the Treble for the fifth time in the club's history

1997........ Win their ninth championship in a row and the League Cup for the 20th time

1999........ Win the Treble for the sixth time

2003........ Win a seventh Treble – including a world record 50th league championship

2005........ Win the Scottish League championship for the 51st time

2006........ First Scottish club in Champions League knock-out stage

❋ RANGERS XI OF THE 1880s ❋

1
Willie
CHALMERS

2
Donald
GOW

3
John
McCARTNEY

4
John
CAMERON

5
Tuck
McINTYRE

6
John
MUIR

7
Hammy
BROWN

8
Andy
PEACOCK

9
Willie
PRINGLE

10
Charlie
HEGGIE

11
Bob
BRAND

Reserves
George *GILLESPIE* • Robert *YOUNG* • *JIM BUCHANAN*
Alick *McKENZIE* • John *GOW*
Honorary Match Secretary
J. *GOSSLAND*

Did You Know That?
Rangers played in the English and Scottish FA Cups in the 1880s.

❋ NINE PAST HAFFEY ❋

Three Rangers players played for Scotland on 15 April 1961 when England beat them 9–3 at Wembley, their record international defeat[†]. Eric Caldow captained Scotland, Davie Wilson won his third cap and Robert Shearer made his international debut in the game. It was only the second game in charge for Scotland's manager, Ian McColl. However, whatever embarrassment the three Rangers players may have felt about the result, it was nothing compared to that of the man between the posts.

'It is reported that Frank Haffey allowed himself to be photographed in front of Big Ben at 9.15pm the same evening of the game. The next morning, his grinning face was plastered all over the papers with Big Ben reading 9–3! Haffey later emigrated to Australia, where he became a nightclub singer and the butt of a joke which went as follows: "What's the time? Nine past Haffey."

✳ RANGERS ON TOUR – 1911 ✳

Kristiansand	Select Grengland v. Glasgow Rangers	0–12 *(w)*
Kristiansand	Select Cristiania v. Glasgow Rangers	0–6 *(w)*
Gothenburg	Orgryte IS v. Glasgow Rangers	2–7 *(w)*
Gothenburg	Select Sweden XI v. Glasgow Rangers	0–3 *(w)*
Copenhagen	Select Denmark XI v. Glasgow Rangers	1–1 *(d)*
Copenhagen	Select Denmark XI v. Glasgow Rangers	1–3 *(w)*

✳ GAZZA THE PRANKSTER (1) ✳

1. He turned up for England training the morning after England's manager at the time, Bobby Robson, had described him as being "as daft as a brush" with a brush sticking out of his socks.
2. He set up his best mate, Jimmy "Five Bellies" Gardner, with a "girl" that Gazza knew was a transvestite.
3. During his time at Middlesbrough, he crashed the team bus at the club's training ground and caused £10,000 worth of damage.
4. On a trip to London, he jumped out of his car and asked a nearby workman for "a go" on his pneumatic drill. After the bemused workman had agreed, Gazza, watched by members of the public, happily proceeded to pound the pavement.
5. When asked for his nationality before an operation, Gazza informed the nurse that he was "Church of England".

✳ TV STARS ✳

Ray Wilkins	Tango Orange advertisement (voiceover)
Paul Gascoigne	Walkers Crisps advertisement
Ally McCoist	Team captain on *A Question of Sport*

✳ GAZZA'S TEARS ✳

When Paul Gascoigne was booked in England's World Cup semi-final game against Germany in the Stadio Delle Alpi in Turin, Italy, on 4 July 1990, he knew that he would miss the final should England win the game. When this realization sank in, Gazza burst into tears, leading to Gary Lineker looking across to the England bench, from where he could clearly be seen mouthing the words "Have a word with him". Of course, England went on to lose the game in a penalty shoot-out and Germany went on to lift the cup after beating Argentina in the final. After the 1990s finals Gazza became a national hero.

✳ JIM BAXTER ✳

James Curran Baxter was born on 29 September 1939 in Hill o'Beath, Fife. Prior to joining Raith Rovers, the club where he began his professional career, he worked down the coal mines. In June 1960, Scot Symon, the Rangers manager, signed Jim from Raith Rovers for £17,500, a record Scottish transfer fee at the time. During his first spell at Ibrox, from 1960 to 1965, "Slim Jim", as he was affectionately dubbed by the Rangers faithful, displayed sublime football skills. However, he broke his leg in Rangers' European Cup away win over Rapid Vienna in December 1964 and the injury kept him out of action for the next three months. When he returned to the Rangers side he was restless and, in April 1965, played what many at the time thought would be his last game for the club in a 1–0 defeat at the hands of Dundee United. In May 1965, he joined Sunderland for £72,500.

Jim never really settled at Sunderland and, less than two years later, he joined Nottingham Forest for £100,000. However, around this time, Jim's off-the-field activities became more noteworthy than his achievements on the pitch and, in 1969, he re-signed for Rangers. Then, in December 1970, Jim unexpectedly announced his retirement from the game that he had graced with such style: he was just 31 years old.

During his Rangers career, Jim won three Scottish League championships, three Scottish Cups and four Scottish League Cups. He also starred for the Scottish national team, winning 34 caps for his country, 24 of them while he was at Rangers. His finest hour in a Scotland shirt came at Wembley on 15 April 1967, when Scotland faced England, the reigning world champions, in a European Championship (1968) qualifying game. Jim loved to take the mickey out of opposing players and was particularly prone in matches involving Scotland and England and Rangers and Celtic. In the game at Wembley, Jim tortured the English World Cup-winning defenders – even having the audacity to play "keepy-uppy" at one point – in Scotland's famous 3–2 victory. The Tartan Army left the stadium proclaiming themselves as the new world champions.

Sometime after he retired, he was asked whether the huge sums of money being paid to footballers after he had already retired from the game would have made a difference to his lifestyle. In typical fashion Slim Jim replied: "Definitely. I'd have spent £50,000 a week at the bookies instead of £100."

Jim died from cancer on 14 April 2001 and fans and former team-mates packed into Glasgow Cathedral to pay their final respects to a true Glasgow Rangers legend.

✸ RANGERS IN EUROPE: 1956–57 TO 1966–67 ✸

Season	Comp.	Round	Opponents	Home	Away	Agg.
1956–57	EC	1st	Nice	2–1	1–2	3–3
			(Rangers lost the play-off in Paris 3–1)			
1957–58	EC	1st	St Etienne	3–1	1–2	4–3
		2nd	AC Milan	1–4	0–2	1–6
1959–60	EC	prelim	Anderlecht	5–2	2–0	7–2
		1st	Red Star	4–3	1–1	5–4
		2nd	Sparta Rotterdam	0–1	3–2	3–3
			(Rangers won the play-off at Highbury 3–2)			
		Sf	Eintracht Frankfurt	3–6	1–6	4–12
1960–61	ECWC	1st	Ferencvaros	4–2	1–2	5–4
		2nd	Borussia Moenchengladbach	2–0	1–1	3–1
		Sf	Wolves	0–2	1–2	1–4
1961–62	EC	prelim	AS Monaco	3–2	3–2	6–4
		1st	ASK Vorwaerts	4–1*	2–1	6–2
			*(*The original home tie was abandoned due to fog (1–0))*			
		Qf	Standard Liege	2–0	1–4	3–4
1962–63	ECWC	1st	Sevilla	4–0	0–2	4–2
		2nd	Tottenham Hotspur	2–3	2–5	4–8
1963–64	EC	prelim	Real Madrid	0–1	0–6	0–7
1964–65	EC	1st	Red Star	3–1	2–4	5–5
			(Rangers won the play-off at Highbury 3–1)			
		2nd	Rapid Vienna	1–0	2–0	3–0
		Qf	Inter Milan	1–0	1–3	2–3
1965–66			Rangers failed to qualify for Europe			
1966–67	ECWC	1st	Glentoran	4–0	1–1	5–1
		2nd	Borussia Dortmund	2–1	0–0	2–1
		3rd	Real Zaragoza	2–0	0–2	2–2
			(Rangers won on the toss of a coin)			
		Sf	Slavia Sofia	1–0	1–0	2–0
		F	Bayern Munich			0–1
			(The final was played in Nuremberg)			

Key: EC – European Cup; ECWC – European Cup-Winners' Cup

✸ TWO FROM TWO FOR STEIN ✸

On 11 December 1968, Colin Stein, making only his second appearance for his country, scored twice in Scotland's 5–0 away win over Cyprus in a World Cup qualifying group seven game. His Ibrox team-mates John Greig and Ronnie McKinnon also played in the match.

❋ WE ARE THE CHAMPIONS (1) ❋

The 1890–91 season did not get off to a great start for Rangers as they went out of the cup at the first hurdle to Celtic. However, their league form was much better, as they won 13, drew three and lost two, scoring 61 goals and conceding 21. Dumbarton pushed Rangers hard all season. Rangers had to win their last game to draw level with Dumbarton at the top of the table and they did so in style, beating Third Lanark 4–1 at Ibrox on 9 May 1891. A play-off between Rangers and Dumbarton was ordered to decide the championship, but the game ended 2–2 and the inaugural Scottish First Division championship was shared.

Scottish Football League
1890–91

	P	W	D	L	F	A	W	D	L	F	A	Pts
=1. Dumbarton	18	7	2	0	35	8	6	1	2	26	13	29
=1. **Rangers**	18	7	1	1	31	11	6	2	1	27	14	29
3. * Celtic	18	7	2	0	26	8	4	1	4	22	13	21
4. Cambuslang	18	5	2	2	30	20	3	2	4	17	22	20
5. * Third Lanark	18	6	0	3	20	15	2	3	4	18	24	15
6. Heart of Midlothian	18	4	2	3	20	15	2	0	7	11	22	14
7. Abercorn	18	4	1	4	20	18	1	1	7	16	29	12
8. St Mirren	18	5	1	3	24	23	0	0	9	15	39	11
9. Vale of Leven	18	5	0	4	19	20	0	1	8	8	45	11
10. * Cowlairs	18	3	2	4	19	27	0	2	7	5	23	6

*Championship play-off: 21 May 1891, Cathkin Park, Glasgow; Dumbarton v Rangers 2–2 (Dumbarton and Rangers declared joint champions); * = 4 points deducted for fielding un-registered players; Renton expelled after 4 games for professionalism, record expunged.*

❋ SCOTLAND'S 50 GREATEST MANAGERS ❋

Bill Struth was named Scotland's third greatest ever manager in a poll conducted by the *Sunday Herald* in 2003, which was won by Jock Stein. Here are all the Rangers greats (managers and players) that are included in the top 50 (their positions in the list are in parenthesis): Sir Alex Ferguson (2), Bill Struth (3), Walter Smith (8), Scot Symon (10), Willie Waddell (11), Graeme Souness (12), Alex McLeish (19), Jock Wallace (20), William Walton (25), Ian McColl (42) and Tommy McLean (45). Walter Smith is the only man to have managed both Rangers and Scotland.

❋ WIT AND WISDOM OF THE BLUES (2) ❋

"I am glad to be joining Rangers and I am proud to be joining Rangers."

***Paul LeGuen** on being announced as Alex McLeish's successor*

❋ RANGERS ON TOUR – 1913 ❋

Copenhagen......Select Denmark XI v. Glasgow Rangers......1–2 *(w)*
Copenhagen......Select Denmark XI v. Glasgow Rangers......1–1 *(d)*

❋ INAUGURAL SPL CHAMPIONS ❋

The new Scottish Premier League was established at the beginning of the 1998–99 season. Rangers were the inaugural winners.

❋ OLD FIRM 2 BELGIUM 0 ❋

Rangers' Ally McCoist and Celtic's Paul McStay scored a goal each in Scotland's 2–0 win over Belgium at Hampden Park on 14 October 1987 in a European Championship qualifying group seven game.

❋ BLOODY BUTCHER ❋

On 6 September 1989, England met Sweden in the Rasunda Stadium, Stockholm, in a World Cup qualifying game. During the first half, Rangers and England centre-back Terry Butcher suffered a cut to the head, but the injury was quickly bandaged and he played on. By the end of the game, the bandage was steeped in blood and his white England shirt was practically red. The game ended 0–0 and virtually guaranteed England's qualification for the 1990 World Cup finals in Italy.

❋ NORTHERN IRELAND 1 RANGERS 6 ❋

No fewer than five Rangers players were in the Scotland side that beat Northern Ireland 6–1 at Windsor Park, Belfast, on 7 October 1961 in a Home Championship game. Eric Caldow, winning his 33rd cap, captained Scotland, while his Ibrox team-mates, Jim Baxter, Ralph Brand (who scored two), Alex Scott (who scored a hat-trick) and Davie Wilson (who scored once) also played. Scotland then beat England and Wales, both in Glasgow and by 2–0, to win the 1962 Home International championship

⚽

❈ UP FOR THE CUP (2) ❈

On their way to the 1894 Scottish Cup final played at Second Hampden Park, Rangers beat Cowlairs 8–0 (h), Leith Athletic 2–0 (h), Clyde 5–0 (a) and Queen's Park 3–1 (a) after a 1–1 home draw. Their opponents in the final were Glasgow Celtic, and this would be the first ever Old Firm Scottish Cup final. Although Celtic were the more experienced team, Rangers had won the previous three Old Firm matches. In the final, played in awful, rainy conditions, the men from Ibrox continued their recent domination by winning 3–1 (scorers: H. McCreadie, Barker and McPherson). Rangers had won the Scottish Cup for the first time: at their 21st attempt.

SCOTTISH FA CUP FINAL
17 FEBRUARY 1894, HAMPDEN PARK, GLASGOW
Rangers (0) 3 v. Celtic (0) 1
(H. McCreadie, Barker, (W. Maley)
McPherson)

Att. 15,000
Rangers: David Haddow, Nicol Smith, Jock Drummond,
Bob Marshall, Andrew McCreadie, David Mitchell, James Steel,
Hugh McCreadie, John Gray, John "Kitey" McPherson, John Barker.

Did You Know That?
One week prior to the final, the grandstand at Celtic Park was severely damaged in a storm with debris being scattered all over the nearby Janefield cemetery. The newspaper stories at the time spoke of Celtic being sued for damages, but nothing ever came of it.

❈ RANGERS ON TOUR – 1921 ❈

Copenhagen......Akademisk BK Copenhagen v. Rangers............0–2 *(w)*
Copenhagen......Boldklubben 1903 Copenhagen v. Rangers.......1–2 *(w)*
Copenhagen......Copenhagen XI v. Rangers..........................1–2 *(w)*

❈ THE BOYS FROM THE BLACKSTUFF ❈

In 1982, while Graeme Souness was still at Liverpool, he appeared in an episode of Alan Bleasdale's television drama *The Boys From The Blackstuff*. He starred alongside his Liverpool team-mate Sammy Lee in the famous scene where Yosser Hughes (played by Bernard Hill) approaches Graeme – playing himself – in a bar and says: "You look like me."

❋ GAZZA THE PRANKSTER (2) ❋

1. One hour after playing in an international for England, he met up with Danny Baker and Chris Evans in a Hampstead pub still wearing his full kit, football boots and all.
2. During his time at Newcastle United, he booked a series of sun-bed sessions for a team-mate, Tony Cunningham. Tony is black.
3. Approached by a reporter and asked for a comment while playing for Lazio, he burped into a television microphone. The club fined him £9,000.
4. He once sent a rose to the Wimbledon dressing room for Vinnie Jones after the infamous testicle-squeezing incident. Vinnie returned the compliment by sending Gazza a toilet brush.
5. During a Glasgow Rangers versus Hibernian game, the referee dropped his yellow card. Gazza picked it up, ran after the referee, stopped him and held the card aloft in the air as if he was booking the referee. The referee did not see the funny side of it, however, and once he had the card back in his hands, booked Gazza!

❋ TWO OUT OF TWO FOR WILLIE ❋

Willie Henderson won his second cap for Scotland in their 5–1 romp over Northern Ireland[†] at Hampden Park on 7 November 1962 in their Home Championship encounter. Henderson's goal, after 76 minutes, was his second in successive games for the Scots, while Manchester United's Denis Law had a field day, scoring four.

❋ EUROPEAN CUP MEDAL WINNERS ❋

Graeme Souness is the only Scot to have played for Rangers who has won a European Cup-winners' medal. Souness won the trophy with Liverpool in 1978, 1981 and 1984.

❋ McCOIST THE PROUD SCOT ❋

Ally McCoist won his first cap for Scotland on 29 April 1986 in a friendly match away to Holland. The game was played at PSV Eindhoven's Phillips Sportpark stadium and ended 0–0. Alex Ferguson was the Scotland manager.

[†]*Future Northern Ireland manager Billy Bingham scored Northern Ireland's goal after just eight minutes to put his team in front.*

❋ RANGERS XI OF THE 1890s ❋

1
David
HADDOW
2
Nicol
SMITH
3
Jock
DRUMMOND
4
Bob
MARSHALL
5
Andrew
McCREADIE
6
David
MITCHELL
7
James
STEEL
8
Hugh
McCREADIE
9
John
GRAY
10
John "Kitey"
McPHERSON
11
John
BARKER

Reserves

David ***REID*** • Neilly ***KERR*** • Neil ***GIBSON***

Tom ***HYSLOP*** • Alec ***SMITH***

Manager

William ***WILTON***

Did You Know That?

Rangers played their first ever League game on 16 August 1890.

❋ EXPERIENCED 'GERS ❋

When Scotland drew 0–0 with Wales at Hampden Park on 22 April 1970 in a Home Championship game, the three Rangers players – John Greig (37 caps), Ronnie McKinnon (22) and Colin Stein (11) – had won a total of 70 caps between them, compared to the 21 won by their eight team-mates that day.

❋ BRIAN LAUDRUP'S DAD BEATS SCOTS ❋

On 9 June 1971, in a European Championship qualifying group five away game in Denmark, Finn Laudrup – the father of future Rangers great Brian Laudrup – scored the only goal of the game in the 43rd minute to sink Scotland in the Idraetsparken, Copenhagen. Rangers' Ronnie McKinnon and Colin Stein were in the Scotland team that day.

⚽

❋ GREIG OWN GOAL SINKS SCOTLAND ❋

John Greig, playing in his 42nd international, scored an own goal to give Northern Ireland a 1–0 win at Hampden Park on 18 May 1971 in a Home Championship game.

❋ BLUES GIVEN A HIDING ❋

On 10 May 1969, England cruised past Scotland 4–1 at Wembley in a Home Championship game in front of 89,902 spectators. England's 1966 World Cup final goalscorers, Geoff Hurst and Martin Peters, ran the Scottish defence ragged, scoring two goals each, with Rangers' Colin Stein scoring Scotland's only goal. John Greig and Willie Henderson were the other Rangers players on view that day.

❋ DOCHERTY SNUBS OLD FIRM PLAYERS ❋

In only his second game as national team manager, Tommy Docherty did not select any Old Firm players for Scotland's friendly against Peru on 26 April 1972[†]. A crowd of 21,001 turned up at Hampden Park to see a relatively inexperienced Scotland side beat the South Americans 2–0.

❋ STEIN BECOMES THE FIRST IN SIX ❋

On 2 July 1972, striker Colin Stein became the first Rangers player to win a cap in six internationals when he replaced Denis Law during Scotland's 0–0 draw with Czechoslovakia in the Brazil Independence Cup at the Estadio Biera Rio, Porto Alegre, Brazil. Manager Tommy Docherty had not picked a single Rangers player in Scotland's previous five internationals.

❋ GREIG LOSES SCOTLAND CAPTAINCY ❋

When John Greig[†] won his 26th cap for Scotland, in their 1–0 friendly win over Denmark at Idraetsparken, Copenhagen, on 16 October 1968, Scotland's manager, Robert Brown, stripped him of the captaincy and handed the captain's armband to Billy Bremner of Leeds United. John won 44 Scotland caps, all of them while he was a Rangers player.

[†]Greig would not captain Scotland again until 22 April 1970, in a 0–0 draw with Wales in a Home Championship game at Hampden Park. It was his 37th international appearance.

❊ WE ARE THE CHAMPIONS (2) ❊

The 1901–02 season saw Rangers hit both the highs and the lows. They won their fourth successive league championship, captured the Glasgow Cup for a third consecutive year and won the coveted Glasgow Exhibition Cup. However, all these successes meant nothing when 25 fans died during the Scotland v. England international at Ibrox Park when a section of the west terracing collapsed. With five games of the season remaining, Celtic needed just five points to clinch the title ahead of Rangers. Amazingly, Celtic lost 1–2 at home to Hearts, 2–3 away to Queen's Park and drew 1–1 with Hibernian at home. Celtic's five-point lead had evaporated and Rangers retained the title by two points.

Scottish League Division One
1901-02

		P	W	D	L	F	A	W	D	L	F	A	Pts
1.	**Rangers**	18	6	1	2	18	16	7	1	1	25	13	28
2.	Celtic	18	5	2	2	19	15	6	2	1	19	13	26
3.	Heart of Midlothian	18	6	2	1	21	8	4	0	5	11	13	22
4.	Third Lanark	18	3	3	3	13	11	4	2	3	17	15	19
5.	St Mirren	18	3	3	3	16	13	5	0	4	13	15	19
6.	Hibernian	18	3	1	5	26	14	3	3	3	10	9	16
7.	Kilmarnock	18	4	2	3	15	10	1	4	4	7	17	16
8.	Queen's Park	18	5	1	3	12	7	0	3	6	9	25	14
9.	Dundee	18	3	3	3	9	9	1	2	6	6	22	13
10.	Morton	18	0	2	7	10	24	1	3	5	10	17	7

❊ WIT AND WISDOM OF THE BLUES (3) ❊

"What can I say about Ally? I love him." *Jorg Albertz, on McCoist*

❊ OLD FIRM 2 NORTHERN IRELAND 1 ❊

No fewer than nine Old Firm players appeared for Scotland as they beat Northern Ireland 2–1 at Hampden Park on 16 November 1966 in a Home Championship and European Championship qualifying group eight game. John Greig, winning his 20th cap, captained Scotland, while his Ibrox team-mates Willie Henderson and Ronnie McKinnon also played. Kilmarnock's Bobby Ferguson, Leeds United's Billy Bremner and six Celtic players completed the team.

✳ PENALTY SHOOT-OUT HIGH AND LOWS ✳

Rangers have played in three European ties that have been settled by a penalty shoot-out, winning two of them and losing one:

UEFA Cup, First Round, 2004–05
Maritimo Funchal (POR) v. Rangers, 1–0 and 0–1
(won 4–2 on penalties)
UEFA Cup, Third Round, 2001–02
Rangers v. Paris Saint-Germain (FRA), 0–0 and 0–0
(won 4–3 on penalties)
UEFA Cup, Third Round, 1999–2000
Rangers v. Borussia Dortmund (GER), 2–0 and 0–2
(lost 1–3 on penalties)

✳ DOCHERTY SNUBS RANGERS AGAIN ✳

In only his fifth game as Scotland manager, Tommy Docherty snubbed Rangers for a second consecutive time when he did not select a single Ibrox player for Scotland's Home Championship game against Northern Ireland at Hampden Park on 20 May 1972. Scotland won the game 2–0.

✳ BRAND'S IRISH TREBLE ✳

Following Ralph Brand's two goals for Scotland in their 4–1 win over Eire at Hampden Park on 3 May 1961, the Rangers man scored again, against the Irish, in Scotland's next international match on 7 May 1961. Scotland won the World Cup qualifying group eight game at Dalymount Park 3–1.

✳ A FISHY TALE ✳

When he was an apprentice at Newcastle United, Paul Gascoigne was so desperate to impress his manager Jack Charlton that he spent a week's wages on fishing equipment and begged Big Jack, a famous angler, to give him a lesson. Big Jack agreed and, when Gazza arrived at the riverbank, he threw everything Gazza had bought, except for the fishing rod, out into the river.

¹Teofilio Cubilas, who played in the game, would become the scourge of Scotland six years later when he scored two goals in Peru's 3–1 mauling of Scotland in their opening game of the 1978 World Cup finals in Argentina. Rangers' Tom Forsyth played in the game in Cordoba on 3 June 1978.

❈ RANGERS XI OF THE 1900s ❈

1
Matt
DICKIE

2
Alex
FRASER

3
Jock
DRUMMOND

4
George
HENDERSON

5
James
STARK

6
Jacky
ROBERTSON

7
Angus
McDONALD

8
Finlay
SPEEDIE

9
Robert
HAMILTON

10
John
WALKER

11
Nicol
SMITH

Reserves
Alex *NEWBIGGING* • Alexander *CRAIG*, George *LAW*
R.S. "Toffee" *McCOLL*
Manager
William *WILTON*

Did You Know That?
Rangers won the first Scottish First Division Championship of the twentieth century in the 1899–1900 season.

❈ NOT VERY CZECH MATE ❈

Six Rangers players were in the Scotland team that stuttered to a 4–0 defeat to Czechoslovakia on 14 May 1961 in a World Cup qualifying group eight game. The match was played in front of a partisan crowd of 48,000 in the Tehelne Pole Stadion, Bratislava.

❈ OLD FIRM PLAYERS NUMBERED ❈

On 17 April 1937 the Scotland team took to the pitch with numbers printed on the back of their shirts for the first time. The Rangers players in the team that beat England 3–1 at Hampden Park were as follows: Jerry Dawson (1), James Simpson (captain) (5), George Brown (6) and Bob McPhail (10), who scored two goals in the game.

❈ RANGERS 2005–06 ❈

The Board

Chairman	David Murray
Vice-Chairman	John McClelland
Chief Executive	Martin Bain
Secretary/Director	Campbell Ogilvie
Director of Finance	David Jolliffe
Director	John Greig
Non-Executive Directors	Alastair Johnston
	David Cunningham King
	Donald Wilson

Coaching Staff

Manager	Alex McLeish
Assistant Manager	Andy Watson
First-Team Coach	Jan Wouters
Under-21 Coach	John Brown
Head of Youth Development	George Adams
Club Captain	Barry Ferguson
Club Doctor	Ian McGuinness
Club Physio	Davie Henderson

❈ IBROX DISASTER 20 YEARS ON ❈

The following article comes from the Rangers' match-day programme of 2 January 1991, the 20th anniversary of the disaster[†]: "A minute's silence will be observed before today's match as a mark of respect to the 66 supporters who tragically lost their lives at Ibrox Stadium on this day, 20 years ago. Willie Waddell wrote at the time: 'These have been black days at Ibrox … days of grief and anguish. The scar is deep.'"

❈ RANGERS' FIRST SCOTLAND CAPTAIN ❈

Donald Gow became the first Rangers player to captain Scotland when he led his country in a 5–0 defeat by England on 17 March 1888 in the Home Championship. It was the only time he captained Scotland.

[†] *Speaking about the disaster, the Rangers captain on the day, and the current Rangers public relations officer, John Greig, said: "Willie Waddell contacted all of the bereaved families to ask permission for players and officials from the club to attend each and every one of the funerals. {It was} an absolutely horrendous time because each individual at the club felt it had happened to their own families."*

❋ UP FOR THE CUP (3) ❋

On their way to the 1903 Scottish Cup final played at Celtic Park, Rangers beat Auchterader 7–0 (h) in the first round, Kilmarnock 4–0 (h) in the second round, Celtic 3–0 (a) in the quarter-finals and Stenhousemuir 4–1 (a) in the semi-finals. The quarter-final tie was the seventh Old Firm derby in the competition, and Rangers had won only one of the previous six. In the final on 11 April 1903, Rangers drew 1–1 with Hearts (James Stark scored Rangers' goal) and the replay, played at the same venue, ended 0–0. The second replay was played on 25 April, again at Celtic Park, and this time Rangers won 2–0 – with goals from Mackie and Hamilton.

SCOTTISH **FA** CUP FINAL (SECOND REPLAY)

25 APRIL 1903, CELTIC PARK, GLASGOW

Rangers (1) **2** v. Heart of Midlothian (0) **0**

(Mackie, Hamilton)

Att. 32,000

Rangers: Matt Dickie, Alex Fraser, Jock Drummond, George Henderson, James Stark, Jacky Robertson, Angus McDonald, Finlay Speedie, Robert Hamilton, Alexander Mackie, Nicol Smith.

Did You Know That?

In the final on 11 April 1903, the game was suspended with just 18 minutes remaining because of poor weather conditions with Rangers leading 1–0. A Bobby Walker goal after the re-start earned Hearts a replay.

❋ SOUNESS 51 DALGLISH 100 ❋

Graeme Souness won his 51st cap for Scotland on 27 March 1986 in a 3–0 friendly win over Romania at Hampden Park. The Scotland goals were scored by Gordon Strachan (18 mins), Richard Gough (27 mins) and Roy Aitken (82 mins). Kenny Dalglish captained Scotland on the night, in his 100th international.

❋ THE THREE AMIGOS ❋

On 13 June 1963, Scotland tore Spain apart, winning 6–2 in a friendly played in Real Madrid's magnificent Estadio Santiago Bernabeu. Rangers' Willie Henderson and Davie Wilson were both on the scoresheet for the Scots, while Jim Baxter also played in the game.

�֍ THE IBROX DISASTER �֍

New Year bells had been ringing,
All of Scotland was singing,
The old year had died,
And the new had been born,
As the news of disaster
From Ibrox came spreading,
The news that would cause
A whole nation to mourn.
Two great goals had been scored,
In the last dying moments.
Jimmy Johnson for Celtic,
For Rangers' young Stein.
Their supporters all cheered them,
With voices of thunder,
Unknowing what waited on staircase 13.
66 people died
Some in the flower of their manhood,
When the fences gave way
And the barriers bent,
Seasoned Glasgow policemen, their faces all tear-stained,
With brave efforts, endeavoured far worse to prevent.
All of Glasgow enjoined,
For the first time in history.
In the Glasgow cathedral no Billys, no Dans
But the Old Firm united to pray for their victims,
Of a tragedy set in the memory of man.
New Year bells had been ringing,
All of Scotland was singing,
The old year had died,
And the new had been born,
As the news of disaster
From Ibrox came spreading,
The news that would cause
A whole nation to mourn.

✖ CALDOW'S SAINTLY TEAM-MATE ✖

On 8 November 1961, Eric Caldow captained Scotland to a 2–0 win over Wales at Hampden Park in a Home Championship game, with Liverpool's Ian St John scoring both goals. Rangers' Jim Baxter, Ralph Brand, Alex Scott and Davie Wilson also played in the game.

❋ THE GLASGOW RANGERS HALL OF FAME ❋

The Glasgow Rangers Football Club Hall of Fame was established in 2000 by chairman David Murray to honour the exploits of Rangers' heroes. Every year since its inception in 2000, more players are added by a panel of experts which includes John Greig, the man voted as Rangers' greatest ever player, and Sandy Jardine – both of whom are members in their own right. To be eligible for nomination, the player has to satisfy five criteria: (1) service to club, (2) number of games played, (3) honours won, (4) international caps and (5) exceptional ability. As at the end of the 2004–05 season, there are 57 members:

Player	App.	Honours	International Caps
Moses McNeil	34	SC (2)	1 (Scot)
Tom Vallance	37	SC (2)	7 (Scot)
John McPherson	218	SL (5), SC (3)	9 (Scot)
Nicol Smith	205	SL (4), (SC 3)	12 (Scot)
Alex Smith	481	SC (4)	20 (Scot)
Tommy Cairns	441	SL (7), SC (2)	6 (Scot)
Andy Cunningham	389	SL (7), SC (1)	12 (Scot)
Bert Manderson	402	SL (6)	5 (N Ire)
Tommy Muirhead	353	SL (8)	8 (Scot)
Sandy Archibald	580	SL (13), SC (3)	8 (Scot)
Alan Morton	440	SL (9), SC (3)	31 (Scot)
David Meiklejohn	563	SL (12), SC (5)	15 (Scot)
Dougie Gray	940	SL (10), SC (6)	10 (Scot)
Bob McPhail	408	SL (9), SC (6)	16 (Scot)
Jimmy Smith	259	SL (5), SC (3)	2 (Scot)
Jerry Dawson	211	SL (5), SC (2)	14 (Scot)
Bobby Brown	296	SL (3), SC (3), SLC (2)	3 (Scot)
Jock Shaw	287	SL (4), SC (3), SLC (2)	4 (Scot)
George Young	428	SL (6), SC (4), SLC (2)	53 (Scot)
Willie Woodburn	329	SL (4), SC (4), SLC (2)	24 (Scot)
Ian McColl	526	SL (6), SC (5), SLC (2)	14 (Scot)
Sammy Cox	310	SL (3), SC (2)	24 (Scot)
Willie Thornton	308	SL (4), SC (1)	7 (Scot)
Willie Waddell	301	SL (4), SC (2)	17 (Scot)
Billy Simpson	239	SL (3), SC (1)	12 (N Ire)
Eric Caldow	407	SL (5), SC (2), SLC (3)	40 (Scot)
Bobby Shearer	407	SL (5), SC (3), SLC (4)	4 (Scot)
Davie Wilson	373	SL (2), SC (5), SLC (2)	22 (Scot)
Ralph Brand	317	SL (4), SC (4), SLC (4)	8 (Scot)

Jimmy Millar	317	SL (3), SC (4), SLC (3)	2 (Scot)
Willie Henderson	426	SL (2), SC (4), SLC (2)	29 (Scot)
Davie Provan	262	SL (1), SC (3), SLC (2)	5 (Scot)
Ronnie McKinnon	473	SL (2), SC (4), SLC (3)	28 (Scot)
Jim Baxter	254	SL (3), SC (3), SLC (4)	34 (Scot)
John Greig	755	SL (5), SC (6), SLC (1), ECWC (1)	5 (Scot)
Sandy Jardine	674	SL (3), SC (5), SLC (5), ECWC (1)	5 (Scot)
Willie Johnston	393	SC (1), SLC (2), ECWC (1)	22 (Scot)
Alex MacDonald	503	SL (3), SC (4), SLC (4), ECWC (1)	1 (Scot)
Colin Stein	206	sLC (2), ECWC (1)	21 (Scot)
Derek Johnstone	546	SL (3), SC (5), SLC (5), ECWC (1)	14 (Scot)
Tommy McLean	452	SL (3), SC (4), SLC (3), ECWC (1)	9 (Scot)
Tom Forsyth	326	SL (3), SC (4), SLC (2)	22 (Scot)
Davie Cooper	540	SL (3), SC (3), SLC (7)	24 (Scot)
Ally McCoist	581	SL (8), SC (1), SLC (9)	61 (Scot)
Ian Durrant	347	SL (3), SC (3), SLC (4)	19 (Scot)
Graeme Souness	73	SL (1)	54 (Scot)
Terry Butcher	176	SL (3), SLC (2)	77 (Eng)
Chris Woods	230	SL (4), SLC (3)	43 (Eng)
Richard Gough	427	SL (9), SC (3), SLC (6)	61 (Scot)
Ray Wilkins	96	SL (2), SLC (1)	84 (Eng)
John Brown	278	SL (6), SC (3), SLC (3)	None
Andy Goram	260	SL (5), SC (3), SLC (2)	48 (Scot)
Brian Laudrup	150	SL (3), SC (1), SLC (1)	61 (Den)
Paul Gascoigne	103	SL (2), SC (1), SLC (1)	57 (Eng)
Mark Hateley	222	SL (5), SC (2), SLC (3)	32 (Eng)
Jorg Albertz	182	SL (3), SC (1), SLC (2)	3 (Ger)
Barry Ferguson	301	SL (4), SC (4), SLC (4)	33 (Scot)

* as of 10 May 2006

Key: SL = Scottish League championship; SC = Scottish FA Cup; SLC = Scottish League Cup; ECWC = European Cup-Winners' Cup

✳ GAZZA PAYS £20 FOR A MARS BAR ✳

Paul Gascoigne once paid £20 for a Mars Bar in a newsagents shop in his hometown of Dunston. He paid for the confectionery with a £20 note and asked the shop owner to keep the change and use it to pay for sweets for the local kids.

❋ RANGERS XI OF THE 1910s ❋

1
Herbert
LOCK

2
George
LAW

3
George
McQUEEN

4
James
GAULT

5
Arthur
DIXON

6
James
WALLS

7
Alexander
ARCHIBALD

8
James
BOWIE

9
Willie
REID

10
Thomas
CAIRNS

11
Alec
SMITH

Reserves
John *HEMPSEY* • George *ORMOND* • David *BROWN*
William *HOGG* • Alex *BENNETT*
Manager
William *WILTON*

Did You Know That?
On 20 November 1915, Rangers played at Falkirk with nine men, losing 2–0. Three players missed their train in Glasgow because of fog.

❋ 40 AND COUNTING ❋

In the same year that Rangers won their 40th Scottish League championship title, 1990, the majestic *QEII* liner returned to the River Clyde to celebrate the 50th anniversary of the foundation of the Cunard Steam Ship Company.

❋ CAPTAIN OF ENGLAND AND RANGERS ❋

Two former Rangers players have captained England: Ray Wilkins (ten games between 22 September 1982 and 24 May 1986) and Terry Butcher[†] (seven games between 12 November 1986 and 4 July 1990).

[†]*Terry Butcher is the only Rangers player to have captained England while he was a Rangers player.*

❋ WIT AND WISDOM OF THE BLUES (4) ❋

"I'll play professional football as long as I can. Then spend the rest of my life being depressed."
Ally McCoist

❋ WARTIME LEAGUES 1940–46 ❋

When war was declared in September 1939, the SFA suspended all football matches and the league was abandoned after just five games. However, only a few weeks after the outbreak of the war an emergency competition was organized. The SFA authorized member clubs to arrange local competitions among themselves. Separate leagues were organized in the south from autumn 1940 and in the northeast from the following year. In 1945–46, the Scottish League resumed responsibility for league competition and operated two national divisions. Wartime championships are unofficial and do not appear in the record books.

Emergency War League 1939–40
Regional League West	Rangers
Regional League East	Falkirk
Championship play-off	Rangers 2 Falkirk 1

Southern League 1941–45
1941	Rangers
1942	Rangers
1943	Rangers
1944	Rangers
1945	Rangers

North-Eastern League 1941–45
1941 *(autumn)*	Rangers Reserves
1942 *(spring)*	Aberdeen
1942 *(autumn)*	Aberdeen
1943 *(spring)*	Aberdeen
1943 *(autumn)*	Raith Rovers
1944 *(spring)*	Aberdeen
1944 *(autumn)*	Dundee
1945 *(spring)*	Aberdeen

Southern League 1945–46
"A" Division:	Rangers
"B" Division:	Dundee

❂ WE ARE THE CHAMPIONS (3) ❂

The 1917–18 season was a dramatic one in Rangers' history. The championship was a hard-fought battle between two evenly matched sides, Rangers and Celtic. Indeed, the destiny of the league championship could not be decided until the very last day of the season: Rangers met Clyde at Ibrox, while Celtic entertained Motherwell at home, with the teams level on 54 points from 33 games played. Rangers won 2–1 and, when Motherwell held Celtic to a 1–1 draw, the championship went to Ibrox for the first time in five years by a single point. Of their 34 league games that season, Rangers won 25, drew six and lost just three times, scoring 66 and conceding 24 goals.

Scottish League
1917–18

		P	W	D	L	F	A	W	D	L	F	A	Pts
1.	**Rangers**	34	15	1	1	42	12	10	5	2	24	12	56
2.	Celtic	34	11	4	2	34	13	13	3	1	32	13	55
3.	Kilmarnock	34	12	2	3	45	16	7	3	7	24	25	43
4.	Morton	34	9	6	2	27	17	8	3	6	26	25	43
5.	Motherwell	34	11	3	3	43	21	5	6	6	27	30	41
6.	Partick Thistle	34	10	4	3	36	19	4	8	5	15	18	40
7.	Queen's Park	34	11	4	2	41	15	3	2	12	23	48	34
8.	Dumbarton	34	8	2	7	24	29	5	6	6	24	20	34
9.	Clydebank	34	7	4	6	30	26	7	1	9	25	30	33
10.	Heart of Midlothian	34	11	1	5	24	15	3	3	11	17	43	32
11.	St Mirren	34	9	6	2	27	12	2	1	14	15	38	29
12.	Hamilton Academicals	34	8	5	4	33	22	3	1	13	19	41	28
13.	Third Lanark	34	6	3	8	29	22	4	4	9	27	40	27
14.	Falkirk	34	8	6	3	29	21	1	3	13	9	37	27
15.	Airdrieonians	34	8	2	7	26	19	2	4	11	20	39	26
16.	Hibernian	34	7	4	6	27	26	1	5	11	15	31	25
17.	Clyde	34	5	2	10	20	32	4	0	13	17	40	20
18.	Ayr United	34	3	4	10	20	28	2	5	10	12	33	19

❂ INTER FAILURE ❂

In the 1964–65 season, Rangers met the Italian champions Inter Milan in the semi-final of the European Cup. Rangers lost 3–1 in the first leg in Milan and won 1–0 at Ibrox, to go out of the competition, 3–2 on aggregate.

✲ PLAY-OFF HIGHS AND LOWS ✲

Rangers have played in three European ties that have been settled by a play-off game, winning two of them and losing one:

European Cup, First Round, 1964–65
Rangers v. Red Star Belgrade (YUG), 3–1 and 2–4
(won play-off 3–1)
European Cup, Quarter-Final, 1959–60
Sparta Rotterdam (NED) v. Rangers, 2–3 and 1–0
(won play-off 3–2)
European Cup, First Round, 1956–57
Rangers v. OGC Nice (FRA) 2–1 and 1–2
(lost play-off 1–3)

✲ RANGERS SIGN JUDAS ISCARIOT ✲

In 1989, former Celtic hero Maurice "Mo" Johnston[†] was playing for Nantes in the French League. Celtic were in negotiations to bring Mo back to Celtic Park, where he had scored 55 goals in 99 games for the Hoops between 1984 and 1987. At the time, Mo had said that if he ever returned to Scottish football, it would be with Celtic, the team he had supported as a boy. Following encouragement from the Celtic board, he even agreed to appear at a live press conference announcing to the world that he was going back home to Celtic. However, enter Rangers and Graeme Souness, who made Mo a financial offer he could not refuse. So, in 1989, Mo Johnston signed for Rangers, a move that infuriated both sets of Old Firm fans. Rangers' fans appeared on television and were seen burning their season tickets and scarves in bitter protest at the signing of not only a Roman Catholic but also a former Celtic player. On the other side of football's religious divide in Glasgow, Celtic fans felt betrayed by their "Prodigal Son" and labelled Johnston the greatest "Judas Iscariot" in football history. Consequently, Mo Johnston became the first big-name Catholic star to play for Glasgow Rangers and the first Catholic signed by the club since the Second World War. When Mo scored his first goal against Celtic for Rangers, he was given a yellow card for over-celebrating. He went on to score 31 goals in 76 games for Rangers between 1989 and 1991.

[†] *Mo once blessed himself after scoring for Celtic against Rangers, the memory of which infuriated the Rangers fans even more when he signed for the club. Later in his career, when he was playing in the North American Major Soccer League for Kansas City, sections of the crowd at away games would still yell out "Judas" and "Traitor".*

❈ TERRY BUTCHER ❈

Terry Butcher was born on 28 December 1958 in Singapore. He began his professional career under Bobby Robson at Ipswich Town and made his debut for the "Tractor Boys" on 15 April 1978 against Everton. For the next eight seasons, Butcher was awesome for Ipswich: a player who inspired others, a great leader and a pillar of defence. He missed out on a place in Ipswich Town's famous 1978 FA Cup-winning team, but did go on to achieve European glory with Ipswich when they lifted the UEFA Cup in 1981.

On 31 May 1980, Ron Greenwood gave Terry his first international cap for England in a 2–1 win over Australia in Sydney. Butcher was part of the England squad that qualified for the 1982 World Cup finals in Spain and was the youngest member of their defence. However, at the end of the 1985–86 season, Ipswich Town were relegated and, after having played in the 1986 World Cup finals in Mexico, Butcher was persuaded to sign for Rangers by Graeme Souness.

Souness made Terry his on-field general and he captained Rangers to three Scottish League championship titles and two Scottish League Cups. Indeed, it was a Terry Butcher header against Aberdeen at Pittodrie that clinched the championship title in 1987. However, early the following season, Terry broke his leg and, as a result, his season, and effectively that of Rangers, was over as Celtic reclaimed the championship and Rangers slipped to third in the league. His injury also ruled him out of the England squad at the 1988 European Championships. However, the following season saw both Terry's return and the return of the Scottish League championship trophy to Ibrox. On 6 September 1989, he played for England in a vital World Cup qualifying game against Sweden in Stockholm and suffered a deep gash to his forehead early in the game. The Rangers man simply asked the England medical team to insert some temporary stitches and place a bandage over the gash. His constant heading of the ball during the game re-opened the wound and, at the end of the 0–0 draw – which guaranteed England's participation in the 1990 World Cup finals in Italy – Terry's once-white England shirt was dripping with blood. At Italia '90, Terry captained England after Bryan Robson went home injured.

After the 1990 World Cup, Terry retired from international football having won 77 caps (32 of them while at Rangers) and having scored three goals. He also quit Rangers later the same year and became the player-manager of Coventry City before becoming player-manager of Sunderland in 1993. In his 176 appearances for Rangers, Butcher was as solid as a rock and an inspirational captain who led by example.

❀ CLUB RECORDS ❀

Record home attendance.................118,567 v. Celtic, 2 January 1939

Record victory...................................13–0 v. Possilpark, Scottish FA Cup,
October 1877

Record League victory....................10–0 v. Hibernian, December 1898

Record defeat...................................2–10 v. Airdrieonians, 1886

Record League defeat.....................0–6 v. Dumbarton, May 1892

Record appearances.........................John Greig, 755, 1960–78

Record League appearances............Sandy Archibald, 513, 1917–34

Record Scottish Cup appearances...............Alec Smith, 74

Record League Cup appearances.................John Greig, 121

Record European appearances........................John Greig, 64

Record goalscorer...........................Ally McCoist, 355 goals, 1983–98

Most goals in one season.................Sam English, 44 goals, 1931–32

Most Scottish Cup goals.................Jimmy Fleming, 44 goals

Most League Cup goals....................Ally McCoist, 54 goals

Most European goals.........................Ally McCoist, 21 goals

Most capped player...........................Terry Butcher, 77 caps for England

Highest transfer fee received............Giovanni van Bronkhorst,
£8.5m, Arsenal, 2001

Highest transfer fee paid...................Tore Andre Flo, £12.5m,
Chelsea, 2000

❀ RANGERS ON TOUR – 1922 ❀

Copenhagen......Copenhagen XI v. Glasgow Rangers.................0–1 *(w)*

Copenhagen......Copenhagen XI v. Glasgow Rangers.................0–3 *(w)*

Copenhagen......Denmark XI v. Glasgow Rangers.....................2–2 *(d)*

❀ RANGERS TO THE RESCUE ❀

England's longest unbeaten streak stands at 20 matches – played
between the 3–2 home loss to Scotland[†] on 13 April 1889 and the
2–1 away loss to Scotland at Celtic Park on 4 April 1896. England's
record during this seven-year streak was 16 wins and four draws (of
the 20 matches, nine of them were played at home). Rangers and
Scotland captain John Drummond played alongside his team-mate
Neil Gibson in the Scotland team that brought England's record
unbeaten streak to an end.

*[†]In the 1800s, Scotland only played three times per year, once each against the other home countries,
England, Ireland and Wales in the Home Championship.*

❋ ANGLO-SCOTTISH DEFEAT FOR RANGERS ❋

In 1981, Rangers took part in the Anglo-Scottish Cup[†] and reached
the quarter-finals, where they were knocked out of the competition
by the eventual winners, Chesterfield. Rangers drew 1–1 at Ibrox
and lost 0–3 away. This was the tournament's final year, as fans grew
disillusioned with it.

❋ OLD FIRM 3 THE DUCHY 0 ❋

In November 1986, Scotland beat Luxembourg 3–0 at Hampden
Park in a 1988 European Championship qualifying game. Two goals
from Davie Cooper and one from Mo Johnston gave Scotland the win
in front of 35,078 fans. Cooper's Ibrox team-mate, Ally McCoist,
won his second cap as a second-half substitute, coming on for Murdo
MacLeod of Celtic.

❋ EMPIRE EXHIBITION TOURNAMENT ❋

The Empire Exhibition Tournament was played in the pre-war
summer of 1938 to mark the Empire Exhibition that was being
held in Bellahouston Park, Glasgow. Eight teams from Scotland
and England participated in the tournament, which took place at
Ibrox Park: Aberdeen, Celtic (the Scottish champions), Hearts and
Rangers represented Scotland with Brentford, Chelsea, Everton and
Sunderland (the English champions) representing England. Everton,
who went on to win the English League championship in 1938–39,
beat Rangers 2–0 to end the host club's interest in the tournament,
which was ultimately won by Celtic.

❋ INTERNAZIONALE OPPONENTS ❋

In the group stage draw for the 2005–06 UEFA Champions League,
Rangers were drawn in the same group as Porto (winners in 1987 and
2004), FC Petrzalka (also known as Artmedia Bratislava, who knocked
Celtic out of the competition that year in the second qualifying round)
and Inter Milan (winners in 1964 and 1965). Rangers qualified from
the group, but lost to Villareal in the first knock-out round.

[†]*The Anglo-Scottish Cup was a tournament arranged for eight of the best teams in both the
English and Scottish Football Leagues during the summer and was competed for from 1976 to
1981. St Mirren were the only Scottish winners of the competition, beating Bristol City 5–1 in
the 1980 final.*

❊ KINGS OF THE SCOTTISH LEAGUE CUP ❊

Rangers have dominated the Scottish League Cup since winning the inaugural competition in 1947. In the 59 finals played, up to and including 2005, Rangers have appeared in 30 of them, lifting the cup 24 times and finishing as runners-up on six occasions. Rangers have beaten Celtic, who are 12 cup wins behind Rangers, in eight finals, but suffered their worst loss in a final to Celtic, when they stuttered to a 7–1 defeat in the 1958 final at Hampden Park.

Year	Venue		Result	
2005	Hampden Park	Rangers	5–1	Motherwell
2003	Hampden Park	Rangers	2–1	Celtic
2002	Hampden Park	Rangers	4–0	Ayr United
1999	Celtic Park	Rangers	2–1	St Johnstone
1997	Hampden Park	Rangers	4–3	Heart of Midlothian
1994	Celtic Park	Rangers	2–1	Hibernian
1993	Hampden Park	Rangers	2–1	Aberdeen
1991	Hampden Park	Rangers	2–1	Celtic *(aet)*
1990	Hampden Park	Aberdeen	2–1	Rangers *(aet)*
1989	Hampden Park	Rangers	3–2	Aberdeen
1988	Hampden Park	Rangers	3–3	Aberdeen
	(Rangers won 5–3 on penalties)			
1987	Hampden Park	Rangers	2–1	Celtic
1985	Hampden Park	Rangers	1–0	Dundee United
1984	Hampden Park	Rangers	3–2	Celtic *(aet)*
1983	Hampden Park	Celtic	2–1	Rangers
1982	Hampden Park	Rangers	2–1	Dundee United
1979	Hampden Park	Rangers	2–1	Aberdeen
1978	Hampden Park	Rangers	2–1	Celtic *(aet)*
1976	Hampden Park	Rangers	1–0	Celtic
1971	Hampden Park	Rangers	1–0	Celtic
1967	Hampden Park	Celtic	1–0	Rangers
1966	Hampden Park	Celtic	2–1	Rangers
1965	Hampden Park	Rangers	2–1	Celtic
1964	Hampden Park	Rangers	5–0	Morton
1962	Hampden Park	Rangers	3–1	Heart of Midlothian
	(Replay)			
1961	Hampden Park	Rangers	2–0	Kilmarnock
1958	Hampden Park	Celtic	7–1	Rangers
1952	Hampden Park	Dundee	3–2	Rangers
1949	Hampden Park	Rangers	2–0	Raith Rovers
1947	Hampden Park	Rangers	4–0	Aberdeen

❊ WIT AND WISDOM OF THE BLUES (5) ❊

"Sorry, Mr Chairman, but this is the earliest I have been late for some time."
Ally McCoist, whose lack of punctuality reached almost legendary status

❊ OLD FIRM CUP FINALS ❊

Since the first Scottish Cup final in 1874, the Old Firm has met in 15 finals with a record of seven victories each and one no contest. Here is a list of Old Firm Scottish FA Cup finals:

2002	Rangers 3–2 Celtic
1999	Rangers 1–0 Celtic
1989	Celtic 1–0 Rangers
1980	Celtic 1–0 Rangers *(aet)*
1977	Celtic 1–0 Rangers
1973	Rangers 3–2 Celtic
1971	Celtic 2–1 Rangers *(replay)*
1969	Celtic 4–0 Rangers
1966	Rangers 1–0 Celtic *(replay)*
1963	Rangers 3–0 Celtic *(replay)*
1928	Rangers 4–0 Celtic
1909	Not awarded[†]
1904	Celtic 3–2 Rangers
1899	Celtic 2–0 Rangers
1894	Rangers 3–1 Celtic

❊ ALFIE CONN'S UNIQUE CUP DOUBLE ❊

Alfie Conn was the first player to win a Scottish FA Cup-winners' medal with both Old Firm teams. He was in the Rangers team that beat Celtic 3–2 in the 1973 final and, in 1977, helped Celtic beat Rangers 1–0.

❊ RANGERS 7 DUNDEE UNITED 1 ❊

On 2 February 2005, Rangers beat Dundee United[††] 7–1 in the Scottish League Cup, their biggest ever win over the club.

[†] *The SFA withheld the cup after a riot at Hampden Park following the drawn replay between Celtic and Rangers.*
[††] *Dundee United were the first Scottish team to play in a UEFA Cup final. They lost the 1987 final 0–1 to IFK Gothenburg.*

✷ WE ARE THE CHAMPIONS (4) ✷

Rangers' 1922–23 championship-winning season began a period when they almost totally dominated Scottish football. Over the following 17 seasons, Rangers would lift the championship 13 times and enjoy six Scottish Cup victories. That season, though, they won the First Division title by five points from Airdrie. On 21 April 1923, Rangers beat Kilmarnock 1–0 at Ibrox, a result that was good enough to secure them their 12th league title. The secret of their success lay in their devastating home form: they won 15 of their 19 home games, drawing the other four. Their away form was not as impressive, though: eight wins, five draws and six defeats.

Scottish League Division One
1922–23

		P	W	D	L	F	A	W	D	L	F	A	Pts
1.	**Rangers**	38	15	4	0	43	11	8	5	6	24	18	55
2.	Airdrieonians	38	14	4	1	41	16	6	6	7	17	22	50
3.	Celtic	38	10	5	4	29	21	9	3	7	23	18	46
4.	Falkirk	38	9	10	0	27	7	5	7	7	17	25	45
5.	Aberdeen	38	10	6	3	28	12	5	6	8	18	22	42
6.	St Mirren	38	11	6	2	32	14	4	6	9	22	30	42
7.	Dundee	38	13	2	4	28	11	4	5	10	23	34	41
8.	Hibernian	38	14	2	3	31	13	3	5	11	14	27	41
9.	Raith Rovers	38	9	8	2	18	14	4	5	10	13	29	39
10.	Ayr United	38	11	6	2	31	45	2	6	11	12	29	38
11.	Partick Thistle	38	11	4	4	33	14	3	5	11	18	34	37
12.	Heart of Midlothian	38	6	10	3	29	20	5	5	9	22	30	37
13.	Motherwell	38	10	6	3	38	24	3	4	12	21	36	36
14.	Morton	38	9	3	7	28	20	3	8	8	16	27	35
15.	Kilmarnock	38	11	1	7	37	26	3	6	10	20	40	35
16.	Clyde	38	10	4	5	24	12	2	5	12	12	32	33
17.	Third Lanark	38	8	5	6	29	22	3	3	13	11	37	30
18.	Hamilton Academicals	38	8	6	5	29	18	3	1	15	14	41	29
19.	Albion Rovers	38	7	3	9	25	22	1	7	11	13	42	26
20.	Alloa Athletic	38	3	7	9	16	29	3	4	12	11	23	23

✷ CHAMPIONS UNDONE BY RUNNERS-UP ✷

In August 2003, Rangers, the Scottish champions, lost 3–0 to Arsenal, the English Premier League runners-up, in a friendly at Ibrox.

❈ DAVIE COOPER ❈

David "Davie" Cooper was born on 25 February 1956 in Hamilton, Scotland. In 1974, having played for Udston United and Hamilton Avondale, Davie began his professional career with Clydebank. From the moment he set foot on a football pitch, Davie Cooper was of a different class to most of the players around him. He possessed a silky touch and his superb raids down the left wing produced hundreds of goals for his team-mates.

In his first season (1974–75) with "The Bankies", Davie scored four times in 26 league games and, in the next, he helped Clydebank to the Scottish Second Division championship, scoring 13 times in 26 league games and attracting the interest of several major clubs south of the border. Arsenal, Aston Villa and Coventry City were all ready with their cheque-books, but Davie wanted to play for Rangers and so stayed with Clydebank in the hope of fulfilling his ambition. During the 1976–77 season, he scored 11 goals in the Scottish First Division and then, in June 1977, Jock Wallace made Davie's dreams come true when he paid £100,000 to bring him to Ibrox.

Davie made his debut for Rangers on 13 August 1977 in a 3–1 defeat at Aberdeen and went on to play in 52 out of Rangers' 53 competitive games that season. He was outstanding and formed a productive partnership with both Derek Johnstone and Gordon Smith. Davie went on to win three Scottish League championships (1977–78, 1986–87 and 1988–89), three Scottish Cups (1978, 1979 and 1981) and an astonishing seven Scottish League Cups (1978, 1979, 1982, 1984, 1985, 1987 and 1988) during his time at the club. However, after 12 seasons at Ibrox, Davie found himself on the fringes of the first team and, in August 1989, he joined Motherwell in a deal worth £50,000. Davie had played 540 games and scored 75 goals for his boyhood heroes and won 20 of his 24 Scottish caps during his Ibrox days.

In 1991, Davie won his fourth Scottish Cup-winners' medal when Motherwell beat Dundee United 4–3 after extra time in the final at Hampden Park. Davie spent five seasons with "The Well" before re-joining Clydebank in 1994. On 22 March 1995, Davie suffered a brain haemorrhage at Broadwood Stadium, Cumbernauld, and passed away the next morning at the tender age of 39. He was still playing professional football at the time and his sudden death stunned the football world. All Scottish football fans were united in paying their respects to one of the finest players ever to have graced the game. His goal against Celtic in the Dryborough Cup final on 4 August 1979, was voted the greatest ever Rangers goal in a poll of fans.

❊ RANGERS – GLASGOW CUP KINGS ❊

For 100 years, between 1888 and 1987, the Glasgow Football Association Cup[†] was contested by senior SFA member clubs in the Glasgow area. The winners received a magnificent globular silver trophy. Unsurprisingly, the Old Firm dominated the competition with 73 wins between them. After the Second World War the Glasgow Cup lost a little of its shine, as the new European competitions started to take precedence. Following Rangers' win in 1971, the competition endured a three-year hiatus before returning for the 1974–75 season, when it was shared for the first time in its history after Celtic and Rangers drew 2–2 in the final. Both Rangers and Celtic always put out their strongest sides whenever it was an Old Firm final. In 1988, the Glasgow Cup was abandoned, but it was later resurrected as an Under-18 tournament.

Glasgow Cup winners

44	Rangers
29	Celtic
6	Partick Thistle
5	Clyde
4	Third Lanark, Queen's Park
1	Cambuslang

Glasgow Cup runners-up

27	Celtic
18	Rangers
14	Clyde
13	Third Lanark
11	Partick Thistle
7	Queen's Park
1	Cowlairs

Glasgow Cup finalists

62	Rangers
56	Celtic
19	Clyde
17	Third Lanark
17	Partick Thistle
11	Queen's Park
1	Cambuslang, Cowlairs

[†]*Rangers lost 3–1 to Cambuslang in the first Glasgow Football Association Cup final in 1888 and beat Celtic 1–0 in the last ever final, in 1987.*

❋ UP FOR THE CUP (4) ❋

On their way to the 1928 Scottish Cup final, Rangers were drawn against a Second Division side in the first three rounds. They beat East Stirlingshire 6–0 (a) in the first round, Cowdenbeath 4–2 at Ibrox in the second round and eased past King's Park in the third round, winning 3–1 at Ibrox. In the quarter-finals, Rangers squeezed past Albion Rovers, winning 1–0 away and, in the semi-final, they beat Hibernian 3–1 at Tynecastle Park. Now only Celtic stood in their way of cup glory. In the final, at a packed Hampden Park on 18 April 1928, Rangers beat Celtic 4–0 to win the cup for the first time since 1903.

SCOTTISH FA CUP FINAL
14 APRIL 1928, HAMPDEN PARK, GLASGOW
Rangers (0) 4   v.   Celtic (0) 0
(Meiklejohn (pen),
Archibald (2), McPhail)

Att. 118,115
Rangers: Tom Hamilton, Dougie Gray, Bob Hamilton,
Jock Buchanan, Davie Meiklejohn, Thomas Craig,
Sandy Archibald, Andy Cunningham, Jimmy Fleming,
Bob McPhail, Alan Morton.

Did You Know That?
At Rangers' 1928 Scottish Cup final banquet celebration, their inspirational captain Davie Meiklejohn, who had scored the opening goal in the final from the penalty spot, declared that now that they had won the cup for the first time in 25 years they could win it again. Rangers went on to lift the cup five times over the following eight years.

❋ RANGERS OVERTAKE CELTIC IN EUROPE ❋

On 28 August 2005, Rangers leap-frogged Celtic in the European Cup top-100 league table following their victory over the Cypriot side Anorthosis Famagusta. Celtic started the 2005–06 season in 13th position with 131 points after 20 seasons of European competition. Rangers were also on 131 points after 24 seasons in Europe, but lay 14th in the table, behind Celtic, on goal difference. However, following Celtic's 0–5 away loss and 4–0 home win against Artmedia Bratislava in their Champions League qualifier, Rangers managed to move above their rivals.

❋ RANGERS GOALKEEPER ALL AT SEA ❋

Rangers' goalkeeper, Stewart Kennedy, was in goal for Scotland when England hammered the Scots 5–1 at Wembley on 24 May 1975[†]. Scotland were already two down, through goals from Gerry Francis and Kevin Beattie, just eight minutes into the game. Colin Bell added a third for England five minutes before half-time, but a Bruce Rioch penalty a minute later briefly restored some hope for the shell-shocked Scottish defence. In the second half, Francis scored again, before David Johnson added a fifth with 15 minutes remaining. The Scotland team that lined up that day was as follows: Kennedy (Rangers), Jardine (Rangers), McGrain (Celtic), Munro (Wolves), McQueen (Leeds), Conn (Spurs), Rioch (Derby), Dalglish (Celtic), Duncan (Hibs) (sub Hutchinson (Coventry)), Parlane (Rangers), MacDougall (Norwich) (sub Macari (Man Utd)).

❋ IBROX HOSTS THE CORONATION CUP ❋

The Coronation Cup was a one-off football tournament to celebrate the coronation of Queen Elizabeth II in 1953. The cup was contested between four English clubs and four Scottish clubs: Aberdeen, Celtic, Hibernian and Rangers (Double winners in 1953) represented Scotland, and Arsenal, Manchester United, Newcastle United and Tottenham Hotspur represented England. All the games were played either at Ibrox Park or Hampden Park. Rangers were knocked out of the tournament by Manchester United (1–2) at Hampden Park on 13 May and Celtic went on to beat Hibernian 2–0 in the final, also played at Hampden, on 20 May.

❋ THE MAGNIFICENT SEVEN ❋

On 12 June 1992, Scotland beat the CIS (Russia) 3–0 in Norrkoping, Sweden, during the 1992 European Championship finals. Seven of the starting line-up for Scotland that day were Old Firm players, while Brian McClair was a former Celtic player. The side to play that day was: Goram (Rangers), McKimmie (Aberdeen), Gough (Rangers), McPherson (Rangers), Boyd (Celtic), McStay (Celtic), McAllister (Leeds United), McCall (Rangers), McClair (Manchester United), McCoist (Rangers), Gallacher (Coventry City). Subs: McInally (Dundee United) for McCoist and Nevin (Everton) for Gallacher.

[†]The defeat ended a run of seven away matches undefeated (two wins and five draws) including the 1974 World Cup finals.

✳ RANGERS XI OF THE 1920s ✳

1
Willie
ROBB

2
Robert
MANDERSON

3
Billy
McCANDLESS

4
Davie
MEIKLEJOHN

5
Arthur
DIXON

6
Tommy
MUIRHEAD

7
Sandy
ARCHIBALD

8
Andy
CUNNINGHAM

9
Bob
McPHAIL

10
Tommy
CAIRNS

11
Alan
MORTON

Reserves
W *MOYLES* • James *MARSHALL* • James *WALLS*
Tommy *MUIRHEAD* • Carl *HANSEN*
Manager
Bill *STRUTH*

Did You Know That?

In the 1920–21 season, Rangers were denied a Scottish League and Cup Double for the second successive season when Partick Thistle beat them 1–0 in the Scottish Cup final at Hampden Park. League winners in 1919–20, Rangers had lost the Cup final 2–0 to Stirling Albion.

✳ RANGERS 2 ENGLAND 0 ✳

On 14 April 1962, Scotland[†] beat England 2–0 in front of 132,441 fans at Hampden Park in a Home Championship game thanks to goals from Rangers' Davie Wilson and Eric Caldow (penalty).

✳ THE LUCK OF THE IRISH ✳

Davie Provan made his debut for Scotland in their 2–1 defeat to Northern Ireland on 12 October 1963 at Windsor Park, Belfast.

†Scotland's win gave them their 20th Home Championship title.

❈ LUCKY COIN TOSS ❈

In the 1966–67 season, Rangers met Real Zaragoza[†] in the quarter-finals of the European Cup-Winners' Cup. Rangers won the home leg 2–0 and lost the away leg by the same score. As the penalty shoot-outs rule did not exist at the time, the referee tossed a coin to decide the winner. Luckily for Rangers, they made the right call.

❈ SPROULE WREAKS HAVOC ON OLD FIRM ❈

On 27 August 2005, Ivan Sproule came on as a substitute against Rangers and scored a hat-trick in Hibs' 3–0 win, the first by a Hibs player at Ibrox in 103 years. Four months earlier, on 30 April 2005, Sproule scored his first goal for Hibs during the game, during the club's shock 3–1 win at Celtic that contributed to Celtic losing the championship to Rangers.

❈ BLUE DISMISSAL ❈

On 6 April 1929, Rangers, who were the league champions, who had lost just one match all season and who were the reigning cup holders, met Kilmarnock in the Scottish Cup final in front of 114,708 fans at Hampden Park. Kilmarnock won the game 2–1, against all the odds, to claim the Scottish Cup for the second time in their history. Just minutes before the final whistle, Buchanan of Rangers became the first player to be sent off in the Scottish Cup final – for ungentlemanly conduct after swearing at the referee.

❈ PITCH BATTLE MARS OLD FIRM CUP FINAL ❈

On 10 May 1980, Rangers lost 1–0 to Celtic after extra time in the Scottish Cup final at Hampden Park. Sadly, the game will be remembered more for the fans fighting on the pitch after the game than for the football that was played during it. Following the game, the police called for all future matches between the Old Firm to be played behind closed doors, and their scheduled meeting in the Glasgow Cup final was postponed.

[†] *Real Zaragoza are one of just three teams to have contested a "domestic" Fairs' Cup final – this was before it became the UEFA Cup. All the teams that did so were Spanish, each appearing in two finals, winning one: 1961–62 Valencia 7–3 Barcelona (two legs); 1963–64 Real Zaragoza 2–1 Valencia (single game); 1965–66 Barcelona 4–3 Real Zaragoza (two legs). Four UEFA Cup finals have been all-Italian affairs, one all-English and one all-West German.*

Scottish FA Cup Finals 1874–1914 (41 Cups)

Winners

10	Queen's Park
9	Celtic
4	Heart of Midlothian, Rangers
3	Vale of Leven
2	Dumbarton, Hibernian, Renton, Third Lanark
1	Dundee, Dumbarton, Falkirk, St Bernard's

1 withheld

Finalists

15	Celtic
12	Queen's Park
10	Rangers
7	Vale of Leven
6	Dumbarton, Heart of Midlothian
5	Renton, Third Lanark
4	Hibernian
2	Clyde
1	Cambuslang, Clydesdale, Dundee, Falkirk,

Scottish FA Cup finals 1920–39 (20 Cups)

Winners

6	Rangers, Celtic
2	Kilmarnock
1	Airdrieonians, Clyde, East Fife, Morton, Partick Thistle, St Mirren

Finalists

9	Rangers
8	Celtic
4	Kilmarnock
3	Motherwell
2	Hibernian, Partick Thistle, St Mirren, East Fife
1	Aberdeen, Airdrieonians, Albion Rovers, Clyde, Dundee, Hamilton Academical, Morton, Third Lanark, Hamilton Academical, Kilmarnock, Raith Rovers, St Bernard's, St Mirren, Thornliebank

Scottish FA Cup finals 1947–2005 (59 Cups)

Winners

21	Rangers
18	Celtic
7	Aberdeen
2	Clyde, Dunfermline Athletic, Heart of Midlothian, Motherwell, St Mirren
1	Dundee United, Falkirk, Kilmarnock

Finalists

30	Rangers
29	Celtic
14	Aberdeen
8	Dundee United
6	Heart of Midlothian
5	Dunfermline Athletic, Hibernian
4	Dunfermline Athletic
3	Airdrieonians, Clyde, Dundee, Kilmarnock, Motherwell, St Mirren
2	Falkirk
1	East Fife, Morton

※ RANGERS' GREATEST EVER TEAM ※

Following an awards ceremony in Glasgow on 21 March 1999, the following team was voted the greatest ever Rangers team after tens of thousands of Rangers fans had cast their votes:

Andy Goram	goalkeeper
John Greig	defender
Sandy Jardine	defender
Terry Butcher	defender
Richard Gough	defender
Jim Baxter	midfielder
Paul Gascoigne	midfielder
Davie Cooper	midfielder
Brian Laudrup	midfielder
Mark Hateley	striker
Ally McCoist	striker

※ RANGERS ON TOUR – 1923 ※

Paris	Cercle Athletique Paris v. Glasgow Rangers	1–6 *(w)*
St Gallen	FC St Gallen v. Glasgow Rangers	0–7 *(w)*
Basel	FC Basle v. Glasgow Rangers	0–3 *(w)*
Paris	French XI v. Glasgow Rangers	1–6 *(w)*
Bern	FC Berne v. Glasgow Rangers	0–7 *(w)*
Geneva	La Chaux de Fonds v. Glasgow Rangers	0–3 *(w)*

※ RANGERS' ANGLOS ※

Seven Glasgow Rangers players have been capped for England (while playing for the club) up to the end of the 2004–05 season. The following lists the players and the number of caps they received during their Ibrox days:

Player	Years	Starts	Subs	Apps	Capt	Goals
Terry Butcher	1986–90	32	0	32	7	0
Chris Woods	1986–91	14	6	20	0	0
Gary Stevens	1988–92	20	0	20	0	0
Trevor Steven	1989–91	4	2	6	0	0
Mark Walters	1991	1	0	1	0	0
Mark Hateley	1992	1	0	1	0	0
Paul Gascoigne	1995–97	21	1	22	0	4
Total		*93*	*9*	*102*	*7*	*4*

❈ WE ARE THE CHAMPIONS (5) ❈

Following five successive Scottish First Division championships, Rangers had lost the 1931–32 title to Motherwell. The following season, they set out to reclaim the one trophy that they coveted above all others. Their pursuit of the title got off to a bad start when they lost 0–1 away to St Mirren, but their league form improved and they only succumbed to one more defeat that season. In the end, Rangers won the title by three points over the previous season's champions. Of the 38 games they played, Rangers won 26, drew ten and lost only twice, scoring 113 league goals and conceding 43.

Scottish League Division One
1932–33

		P	W	D	L	F	A	W	D	L	F	A	Pts
1.	Rangers	38	14	5	0	67	22	12	5	2	46	21	62
2.	Motherwell	38	15	1	3	66	24	12	4	3	48	29	59
3.	Heart of Midlothian	38	15	3	1	49	16	6	5	8	35	35	50
4.	Celtic	38	13	3	3	47	18	7	5	7	28	26	48
5.	St Johnstone	38	15	2	2	47	17	2	8	9	23	38	44
6.	Aberdeen	38	13	4	2	63	19	5	2	12	22	39	42
7.	St Mirren	38	12	3	4	48	23	6	3	10	25	37	42
8.	Hamilton Academicals	38	11	5	3	54	31	7	1	11	36	47	42
9.	Queen's Park	38	11	5	3	46	24	6	2	11	32	55	41
10.	Partick Thistle	38	9	3	7	47	28	8	3	8	28	27	40
11.	Falkirk	38	9	5	5	46	25	6	1	12	24	45	36
12.	Clyde	38	12	0	7	42	29	3	5	11	27	46	35
13.	Third Lanark	38	12	3	4	47	27	2	4	13	23	53	35
14.	Kilmarnock	38	8	5	6	45	39	5	4	10	27	47	35
15.	Dundee	38	9	6	4	34	27	3	3	13	26	50	33
16.	Ayr United	38	11	2	6	41	28	2	2	15	21	67	30
17.	Cowdenbeath	38	9	3	7	44	38	1	2	16	21	73	25
18.	Airdrieonians	38	9	2	8	37	34	1	1	17	18	68	23
19.	Morton	38	4	3	12	29	42	2	6	11	20	55	21
20.	Stirling Albion	38	6	3	10	30	44	1	0	18	25	71	17

❈ WIT AND WISDOM OF THE BLUES (6) ❈

"No comment lads – and that's off the record."
Ally McCoist, during a club media ban

❋ FAMOUS DERBIES ❋

The Old Firm derby is just one of many famous football derbies across the world. Others include:

Hibernian v. Heart of Midlothian (Scotland)
Manchester United v. Manchester City (England)
Everton v. Liverpool (England)
Tottenham Hotspur v. Arsenal (England)
AC Milan v. Inter Milan (Italy)
Lazio v. Roma (Italy)
Boca Juniors v. River Plate (Argentina)
Al-Ahly v. Zamalek (Egypt)
Fenerbahce v. Galatasaray (Turkey)
Hapoel Tel-Aviv v. Maccabi Tel-Aviv (Israel)
Colo Colo v. Universidad Catolica (Chile)
Lodz v. Widzew Lodz (Poland)
Independiente Santa Fe v. Millonarios (Colombia)
CSKA Moscow v. Spartak Moscow (Russia)
Levski Sofia v. Slavia Sofia (Bulgaria)
Flamengo v. Fluminese (Brazil)
Legia Warsaw v. Polonia Warsaw (Poland)
Sarajevo v. Zeljeznicar (Bosnia)
Red Star Belgrade v. Partizan Belgrade (Serbia and Montenegro)
Olympiakos Piraeus v. Panathinaikos (Greece)
Aris Salonika v. PAOK Salonika (Greece)
PFC Botev Plovdiv v. PFC Lokomotiv Plovdiv (Bulgaria)
Flamengo v. Vasco da Gama (Brazil)
Botafogo v. Fluminese (Brazil)
Sao Paolo v. Palmeiras (Brazil)
Independiente v. Racing Club (Argentina)
Estudiantes v. Gimnasia (Argentina)
Independiente Medelin v. Atletico Nacional (Colombia)
America de Cali v. Deportivo de Cali (Colombia)
Barcelona v. Espanyol (Spain)
Atletico Madrid v. Real Madrid (Spain)
Betis Sevilla v. Sevilla (Spain)
Athletic Bilbao v. Real Sociedad (Spain)
Las Palmas v. Tenerife (Spain)
Genoa v. Sampdoria (Italy)
Glentoran v. Linfield (Northern Ireland)
Bohemians v. Shamrock Rovers (Republic of Ireland)
Juventus v. Torino (Italy)

❋ IAN DURRANT ❋

Ian Durrant was born on 29 October 1966 in Glasgow. He began his professional career with his boyhood heroes, Rangers, after joining them straight from school. He worked his way through the youth system at Ibrox and, on 20 April 1985, made his Rangers debut in a 3–0 away win at Greenock Morton. He was just 18 years old and went on to make four further league appearances that season. The following season he had become a regular in the Rangers starting XI and he scored his first goal for the club in his first Old Firm derby.

By the time Graeme Souness had arrived as the new manager of Rangers in the summer of 1986, Durrant's place in the team was guaranteed. In the 1986–87 season, he played in 39 of Rangers' league games, helping them to the Scottish Premier League title, and threw four goals in for good measure. He also helped Rangers to Scottish League Cup success that year and scored the opening goal in the 2–1 final victory against Celtic.

On 8 October 1988, following a tackle by Neil Simpson in a match against Aberdeen at Pittodrie, Durrant suffered a horrific knee injury that kept him out of action for almost two-and-a-half years. He was 21 years old at the time of the injury and had a promising career ahead of him both with Rangers (for whom he had already made 122 appearances) and Scotland. Durrant simply had it all: a delicate touch, finesse, consummate skill and the ability to finish off a chance when it was presented to him in front of goal. He was the lynchpin in the Rangers midfield and the supplier of many slide-rule passes which put Ally McCoist in behind opposing defences to score.

On 6 April 1991, Ian Durrant made his long-awaited first-team comeback against Hibernian: 15,000 fans had previously turned up at Ibrox to watch his comeback game in the reserves. The following season, Durrant was at the heart of everything good about Rangers as they marched on an unbeaten 44-game run and came within touching distance of the 1993 Champions League final.

Durrant was a key figure in Rangers' run of nine successive Scottish League championships, with the record-equalling ninth coming in 1997. During his Ibrox career, Ian won three Scottish League championships, three Scottish Cups and four Scottish League Cups, making a total of 347 appearances (scoring 45 goals), although this could have been closer to 500 had it not been for his injury. He left Rangers in 1998 to join Kilmarnock, where he spent two years before becoming their youth team coach. He later returned to Rangers as an Under-19 coach.

❈ THE BLUE SEA OF IBROX ❈

I have sailed the wild Atlantic
Crossed the broad Pacific shore
I've sailed around the stormy capes
And heard the forties' roar
I've plied the Indian Ocean
I've sailed the China Sea
But there's a sea back home in Scotland
More than all the rest to me
It's the blue blue blue sea of Ibrox
It's the greatest sight
That I have ever seen
It's the blue blue blue sea of Ibrox
And it's part of every
Rangers players' dream
No more I'll sail the Seven Seas
No more I'll ever roam
No more I'll feel the urge again
I'm back where I belong
At three o'clock each Saturday
I'll join the mighty throng
With flags and banners all around
I'll proudly sing this song
It's the blue blue blue sea of Ibrox
It's the greatest sight
That I have ever seen
It's the blue blue blue sea of Ibrox
And it's part of every
Rangers players' dream.

❈ RANGERS' BACKERS UNDER INVESTIGATION ❈

On 19 November 1997, UEFA announced that they were to launch an investigation into ENIC, the company that invested £40 million in Rangers during the 1996–97 season. ENIC had already arranged a meeting between the six European clubs it was involved with in Glasgow at the beginning of December and it was believed that UEFA was concerned that the meeting was the first step by ENIC to carve up European football. UEFA spokesman Massimo Gonnella said: "The meeting of these clubs in Glasgow is just a single example, so it is difficult to say how UEFA will treat it. That is why we are holding the investigation."

❄ UP FOR THE CUP (5) ❄

Rangers blasted Blairgowie 14–2 at Ibrox in the first round of the 1933–34 Scottish Cup, equalling their record score (they beat Whitehill 14–2 in the cup on 29 September 1883). In the second round, they beat Third Lanark 3–0 at Cathkin Park and defeated Hibs 2–1 at Tynecastle in the third round in a replay. Aberdeen were beaten 1–0 in the quarter-finals at Ibrox; then St Johnstone succumbed to the same scoreline in the semi-final played at Hampden Park. In the final, also played at Hampden Park, on 21 April 1934, Rangers blasted St Mirren 5–0 in front of 113,403 fans. Four days later, Rangers beat Falkirk 3–1 at Brockville in the Scottish League to clinch the Double.

SCOTTISH FA CUP FINAL
21 APRIL 1934, HAMPDEN PARK, GLASGOW
Rangers (2) **5**   v.   St Mirren (0) **0**
(Nicholson (2), McPhail,
Main, Smith)
Att. 113,403
Rangers: Tom Hamilton, Dougie Gray, Whitey McDonald, Davie Meiklejohn, Jimmy Simpson, George Brown, F.R. Main, James "Doc" Marshall, George Stevenson, Bob McPhail, Willie Nicholson.

Did You Know That?
Jimmy Fleming scored nine of Rangers' 14 goals in their 14–2 mauling of Blairgowie, a record for the Scottish Cup.

❄ McCOIST HUNGARY FOR SUCCESS ❄

On 9 September 1987, Scotland beat Hungary 2–0 in a friendly at Hampden Park[†], with Ally McCoist, playing in his seventh international, netting his first two goals for his country.

❄ 14-UP ❄

In the 1924–25 season, Rangers collected their 14th Scottish First Division championship title. It was the 12th time they had finished on top of the table in the 20th century.

'Blues' Ian Durrant won his first cap in the game, while a future Rangers player, Mo Johnston (FC Nantes), also played.

❄ FAMOUS OLD FIRM QUOTE ❄

Mo Johnston, who played for both Old Firm sides, once famously said: "For a while I did unite Rangers and Celtic fans. There were people in both camps that hated me."

❄ FOUR OFF IN OLD FIRM CLASH ❄

Four players were sent off when Rangers played Celtic in the 1991 Scottish Cup: Terry Hurlock, Mark Walters and Mark Hateley of Rangers and Peter Grant of Celtic.

❄ RANGERS NICKNAMES ❄

Rangers are nicknamed "The 'Gers" or "The Teddy Bears".

❄ NEW MANAGER LOYAL TO THE OLD FIRM ❄

In his first match in charge of Scotland, Malcolm MacDonald selected seven Old Firm players for their Home Championship and European Championship qualifying group eight game against Wales at Ninian Park, Cardiff, on 22 October 1966. The game ended 1–1, with Denis Law scoring for Scotland. The Rangers players on show that day were John Greig, Ronnie McKinnon and Willie Henderson[†].

❄ OLD FIRM 1 WORLD CHAMPIONS 1 ❄

Scotland, featuring no fewer than eight Old Firm players, drew 1–1 with world champions England at Hampden Park in front of a crowd of 134,000 on 24 February 1968 in a Home Championship and European Championship qualifying group eight game. The Rangers players on view that day were Ronnie McKinnon, John Greig (who captained the side) and Willie Johnston.

❄ RANGERS BEAT BIBLICAL TEAM ❄

In the 1933–34 season, Queen of the South, the only senior British football club whose name appears in the Bible (*Matthew* 12:42) played in the top flight for the first time. Despite getting off to a dream start by beating Celtic 3–2 in their opening fixture, they lost to Rangers 1–5 at Ibrox and 0–4 at home.

[†]*Rangers legend Jim Baxter, then at Sunderland, also played in the game.*

✳ RANGERS XI OF THE 1930s ✳

1
Jerry
DAWSON

2
Dougie
GRAY

3
Jock
BUCHANAN

4
Davie
MEIKLEJOHN

5
Jimmy
SIMPSON

6
George
BROWN

7
Totty
GILLICK

8
Alec
VENTERS

9
Jimmy
SMITH

10
Bob
McPHAIL

11
Dave
KINNEAR

Reserves
Tom *HAMILTON* • J *KENNEDY* • Sammy *ENGLISH*
Bob *McDONALD* • Jimmy *FLEMING*
Manager
Bill *STRUTH*

Did You Know That?
Rangers completely dominated Scottish football in the 1930s, winning
seven league titles, five Scottish Cups, and the Double three times.

✳ WIT AND WISDOM OF THE BLUES (7) ✳

"The Italians are known for that, boss. Fowl play."
*Ally McCoist, after manager Graeme Souness told of the plan to poison
Trevor Francis's chicken dinner*

✳ RANGERS ON TOUR – 1933 ✳

Berlin	Germany XI v. Glasgow Rangers	1–5 *(w)*
Hamburg	Germany XI v. Glasgow Rangers	1–3 *(w)*
Bochum	Germany XI v. Glasgow Rangers	0–5 *(w)*
Dresden	Germany XI v. Glasgow Rangers	2–3 *(w)*
Munich	Germany XI v. Glasgow Rangers	2–1 *(l)*
Vienna	Rapid Vienna v. Glasgow Rangers	4–3 *(l)*

❈ FOUR BEHIND ❈

In the 1922–23 season, Rangers won their 12th Scottish First Division championship title to move four behind Celtic in the list of most frequent winners.

❈ A NIGHT OF SHAME ❈

On 21 May 1969, Rangers lost 2–0 at St James' Park to Newcastle United in the second leg of their Fairs' Cup semi-final tie. The result meant that the Geordies advanced to the final having drawn the first leg 0–0 at Ibrox. However, the game is remembered more for the incidents that occurred off the field than for the football that was played on it. When Jackie Sinclair scored Newcastle United's second goal in the 77th minute, all hell broke loose on the terraces occupied by the Tartan Army from Glasgow. Hundreds of Rangers fans poured out of the Gallowgate End and onto the pitch. A "riot" quickly ensued, with bottles and beer cans being thrown, and fighting broke out between the Rangers fans, not only with the police but also with one another. The referee, John Gow, quite sensibly took the players off the field and into the tunnel area where they remained for almost 20 minutes as the outnumbered police struggled to restore order. When the game was finally re-started, a continuous line of blue police uniforms was present from one corner flag to the other. Police dogs and horses were also quickly brought into the ground to prevent any further trouble.

❈ THE OLD FIRM'S SCOTTISH CUP DYNASTY ❈

Since the Scottish FA Cup resumed after the Second World War, there have only been 11 occasions, between 1947 and 2006, when the Old Firm has not been represented in the final:

2006	Hearts 1–1 Gretna *(aet, Hearts 4–2 pens)*
1997	Kilmarnock 1–0 Falkirk
1991	Motherwell 4–3 Dundee United *(aet)*
1987	St Mirren 1–0 Dundee United *(aet)*
1986	Aberdeen 3–0 Hearts
1968	Dunfermline 3–1 Hearts
1959	St Mirren 3–1 Aberdeen
1958	Clyde 1–0 Hibernian
1957	Falkirk 2–1 Kilmarnock *(aet, replay)*
1952	Motherwell 4–0 Dundee
1947	Aberdeen 2–1 Hibernian

❉ WEMBLEY WIZARDS ❉

On 31 March 1928, Scotland unceremoniously thrashed England 5–1 at Wembley in front of 80,868 to earn them the legendary title "The Wembley Wizards"[†]. Rangers' Alan Morton was Scotland's most experienced player, winning his 19th cap in the game. The Scotland team to line up that day was: John Diamond Harkness (Queen's Park), James Nelson (Cardiff City), Thomas Law (Chelsea), James Davidson Gibson (Aston Villa), Thomas Bradshaw (Bury), James McMullan (captain, Manchester City), Alexander Skinner Jackson, (Huddersfield Town), James Dunn (Hibernian), Hugh Kilpatrick Gallacher (Newcastle United), Alexander Wilson James (Preston North End), Alan Lauder Morton (Rangers).

❉ LAST-GASP WINNERS ❉

On the final day of the 2004–05 season, Rangers pipped Celtic to the Scottish Premier League title. Going into their match at Motherwell, Celtic were two points ahead of Rangers in the table and, at the start of the day, Celtic led Motherwell thanks to a Chris Sutton strike. However, two goals in the closing minutes from Scott McDonald earned Motherwell a 2–1 win, meaning that Nacho Novo's goal that gave Rangers a 1–0 win over Hibernian also gave them the League championship by a single point.

❉ SCOTLAND'S PFA PLAYER OF THE YEAR ❉

At the end of every Scottish football season, the members of the Scottish Professional Footballers' Association vote to decide which one of its union members has played the best football during the season. The award was first given in 1978 and went to Rangers' Derek Johnstone. Here is a list of the eight other Rangers players who followed Derek:

Ally McCoist (1992) ❖ Andy Goram[††] (1993)
Mark Hateley (1994) ❖ Brian Laudrup (1995)
Paul Gascoigne (1996) ❖ Lorenzo Amoruso (2002)
Barry Ferguson (2003) ❖ Fernando Ricksen[†††] (2005)

[†]*William Bell of Scotland refereed the game. Surprisingly, Hughie Gallacher failed to score, with Jackson grabbing a hat-trick and James netting the other two goals.*

[††]*Andy Goram was the first, and to date only, goalkeeper to receive the award, and Richard Gough, a future Rangers player, won it in 1986 when he was at Dundee United.*

[†††]*Fernando Ricksen shared the award with Celtic's John Hartson.*

❈ RANGERS' FIRST ULSTERMAN ❈

Bert Manderson was the first Northern Ireland born player to captain Rangers Football Club. He signed for Rangers in 1915, costing £150, and went on to win six Scottish First Division Championships, six Glasgow Cups, four Glasgow Charity Cups and the Lord Provost's Rent Relief Cup in 1921–21 during his 12 years with the club.

❈ CZECH MATE ❈

On 26 September 1961, Scotland gained revenge for their 4–0 defeat by Czechoslovakia in Bratislava five months earlier by beating the Czechs 3–2 at Hampden Park in a World Cup qualifying group eight match. Eric Caldow captained the side that included his Ibrox team-mates Jim Baxter, Alex Scott and Davie Wilson.

❈ RANGERS 17 CELTIC 17 ❈

In the 1962–63 season, Rangers drew level with Celtic in the table for the highest number of Scottish FA Cup wins. Both Old Firm teams had now won the Scottish Cup 17 times[†].

❈ OLD FIRM RIOT AT 1909 CUP FINAL ❈

At the 1909 Scottish FA Cup final replay at Hampden Park, Rangers and Celtic fans ran riot at the end of the match following the second drawn game between the two sides. Both on the pitch and in the terraces, players and fans had assumed that extra time would be played to decide a winner. However, under SFA rules at the time, extra time was only permissible at the end of a second replay. When the referee told the players to leave the pitch, the 60,000-strong crowd inside Hampden Park went crazy, believing that the two drawn games had been staged by the clubs to bring in additional revenue. Hundreds of fans ran onto the pitch and vented their anger by tearing down the goals, cutting up the turf and setting fire to the turnstiles and Main Stand using whisky as fuel. Over 100 people were hurt during the rioting, many of them policemen and firemen. In the aftermath of the rioting, the SFA took the decision to withhold both the cup and the players' medals, and both clubs were ordered to pay the appropriate amount of compensation to Queen's Park Football Club, the owners of Hampden Park.

[†]*Rangers successfully defended the cup the following year to move one ahead of Celtic in the table of cup winners.*

✼ RANGERS PLAY BEHIND CLOSED DOORS ✼

On 29 September 2005, Rangers played Inter Milan in the Giuseppe Meazza Stadium (known as the San Siro when AC Milan play their home matches there) in a Champions League group game and lost 1–0. Inter were ordered by UEFA to play their first four Champions League home games of 2005–06 behind closed doors following the crowd disturbances that marred their Champions League quarter-final exit to bitter rivals AC Milan at the stadium the previous season[†].

✼ BEFORE RANGERS ✼

The following Rangers players/managers all had another occupation before football:

Marvin Andrews	A brewer in Trinidad
Jim Baxter	Miner
Davie Cooper	Printer
Sir Alex Ferguson CBE	Toolmaker
Dado Prso	Mechanic
Willie Rae	Quantity surveyor
Walter Smith	Electrician
Billy Williamson	Royal Navy PE teacher

✼ EDWARDIAN KINGS ✼

For the first 14 seasons of the 20th century, up to the outbreak of the First World War, the Old Firm dominated Scottish football. During these years, Celtic won the Scottish First Division seven times and the Scottish Cup six times. Rangers won the league five times and the Scottish Cup once. The closest any club came to challenging their monopoly was Hibernian, who won one league championship and one Scottish Cup, while Heart of Midlothian managed two Scottish Cup final victories.

✼ BUDDIES' RECORD DEFEAT ✼

On 4 December 1897, St Mirren ("The Buddies") suffered their record defeat when they lost 9–0 to Rangers at Ibrox.

[†] *As the only people permitted to attend the game were the two teams, stadium officials, UEFA officials, the media and approximately 200 fans from each side, it is the lowest "crowd" that Rangers have ever played in front of.*

❋ WE ARE THE CHAMPIONS (6) ❋

The 1948–49 season will go down in history as Rangers became the first Scottish team to win the "Triple Crown" (or the "Treble" as it is known today) of league championship, Scottish FA Cup and Scottish League Cup. In the league, Dundee pushed Rangers all the way to the last day: the men from Ibrox visited Coatbridge while Dundee travelled to Falkirk needing just a draw to win the title as they had 45 points to Rangers' 44. As Dundee crashed to a 1–4 defeat at Falkirk, Rangers hammered Coatbridge by the same score to clinch the championship by a single point.

Scottish League 'A' Division
1948–49

		P	W	D	L	F	A	W	D	L	F	A	Pts
1.	Rangers	30	11	3	1	39	18	9	3	3	24	14	46
2.	Dundee	30	13	1	1	41	20	7	4	4	30	28	45
3.	Hibernian	30	9	3	3	37	20	8	2	5	38	32	39
4.	East Fife	30	9	1	5	39	19	7	2	6	25	27	35
5.	Falkirk	30	9	3	3	44	23	3	5	7	26	31	32
6.	Celtic	30	7	3	5	26	17	5	4	6	22	23	31
7.	Third Lanark	30	9	2	4	33	22	4	3	8	23	30	31
8.	Heart of Midlothian	30	8	2	5	37	22	4	4	7	27	32	30
9.	St Mirren	30	9	3	3	30	16	4	1	10	21	31	30
10.	Queen of the South	30	8	3	4	28	19	3	5	7	19	34	30
11.	Partick Thistle	30	4	8	3	25	24	5	1	9	25	39	27
12.	Motherwell	30	7	2	6	29	20	3	3	9	15	29	25
13.	Aberdeen	30	5	4	6	26	26	2	7	6	13	22	25
14.	Clyde	30	5	4	6	27	30	4	2	9	23	37	24
15.	Morton	30	4	6	5	21	22	3	2	10	18	29	22
16.	Albion Rovers	30	3	1	11	18	44	0	1	14	12	61	8

❋ GREIG TAKES ON PELE ❋

On 25 June 1966, Rangers' John Greig captained Scotland against Brazil in a friendly in front of 74,933 fans at Hampden Park. Celtic's Stevie Chalmers scored a goal in less than a minute for Scotland, but the game ended 1–1 with Servilo scoring an equalizer for the two-time World Cup winners in the 15th minute. Greig's Ibrox team-mate Ronnie McKinnon also played in the game. Brazil, warming up for the 1966 World Cup finals, failed to qualify from their group.

❋ PAUL GASCOIGNE ❋

Paul John Gascoigne was born in Gateshead, County Durham on 27 May 1957. He grew up in the Dunston area of Gateshead and first played for Redheugh Boys Club. In 1983, he signed as an apprentice with Newcastle United following his failure to impress in trials with Ipswich Town, Middlesbrough and Southampton. Gazza made his Newcastle United debut in 1985 and went on to make a total of 107 appearances for the Geordies, scoring 25 times.

In 1988, Gazza was lured to Tottenham Hotspur in a deal worth £2 million. On 14 September 1988, he made his international debut for England when he came on as a substitute in England's 1–0 friendly win over Denmark at Wembley. Paul went on to play 57 times for his country, scoring 10 goals, and will always be remembered for bursting into tears after he was booked in England's World Cup semi-final defeat by Germany at Italia '90. Later in 1990, he was named the BBC's "Sports Personality of the Year".

In 1991, Gazza won the FA Cup with Spurs but a proposed move to SS Lazio was put on hold when he suffered a knee injury in the final. Following a year out of the game, Gazza finally moved to the Italian side in the summer of 1992 for £5.5 million. Gazza could not cope with his "fishbowl-like" existence in Serie A and, in June 1995, he signed for Rangers. He was an instant hit with the Ibrox faithful, getting booked against Celtic for playing an imaginary flute after scoring in an Old Firm win. At the end of the 1995–96 SPL season, he scored a hat-trick in the penultimate league game against Aberdeen, helping Rangers to the SPL title. He was named the "Scottish Player of the Year" for season 1995–96.

Gazza left Rangers for Middlesbrough at the end of the 1997–98 season after securing two Scottish Premier League winners' medals, one Scottish Cup victory and one Scottish League Cup success. In total, Gazza played 103 times for Rangers, scoring 39 goals. The Rangers fans will always hold a special place in their hearts for the player the England manager, Bobby Robson, described as being "as daft as a brush". Gazza was one of the greatest players ever to wear a Rangers shirt, a maverick footballer who made fans stand up when he was in possession of the ball in anticipation of what he was about to do next.

After Middlesbrough, Gazza joined Everton (2000–02), Burnley (2002), Gansu Tianma (China – 2003) and Boston United (2004–05). Gazza also had unsuccessful spells in management with Algarve United (Portugal) and Kettering Town. In 2002, Gazza was inducted into the English Football Hall of Fame.

❋ RANGERS' SCOTTISH CUP HISTORY ❋

Apart from their 15 Scottish Cup finals against Celtic, seven of which they won, Rangers have also appeared in 34 other Scottish Cup finals, winning 24 of them:

2003	Rangers 1–0 Dundee
2000	Rangers 4–0 Aberdeen
1998	Hearts 2–1 Rangers
1996	Rangers 5–1 Heart of Midlothian
1994	Dundee United 1–0 Rangers
1993	Rangers 2–1 Aberdeen
1992	Rangers 2–1 Airdrieonians
1983	Aberdeen 1–0 Rangers *(aet)*
1982	Aberdeen 4–1 Rangers *(aet)*
1981	Rangers 4–1 Dundee United *(replay)*
1979	Rangers 3–2 Hibernian *(aet, second replay)*
1978	Rangers 2–1 Aberdeen
1976	Rangers 3–1 Heart of Midlothian
1964	Rangers 3–0 Dundee
1962	Rangers 2–0 St Mirren
1960	Rangers 2–0 Kilmarnock
1953	Rangers 1–0 Aberdeen *(replay)*
1950	Rangers 3–0 East Fife
1949	Rangers 4–1 Clyde
1948	Rangers 1–0 Morton *(aet, replay)*
1936	Rangers 1–0 Third Lanark
1935	Rangers 2–1 Hamilton Academical
1934	Rangers 5–0 St Mirren
1932	Rangers 3–0 Kilmarnock *(replay)*
1930	Rangers 2–1 Partick Thistle *(replay)*
1929	Kilmarnock 2–0 Rangers
1922	Morton 1–0 Rangers *(aet, replay)*
1921	Partick Thistle 1–0 Rangers
1905	Third Lanark 3–1 Rangers *(replay)*
1903	Rangers 2–0 Heart of Midlothian *(second replay)*
1898	Rangers 2–0 Kilmarnock
1897	Rangers 5–1 Dumbarton
1879	Vale of Leven 1–1 Rangers *(Vale of Leven awarded cup when Rangers failed to turn up for the replay)*
1877	Vale of Leven 3–2 Rangers *(replay)*

❈ UP FOR THE CUP (6) ❈

On 23 April 1949, Rangers completed the second leg of that season's magnificent Treble by beating Clyde 4–1 in the Scottish Cup final at Hampden Park (Rangers had already collected the Scottish League Cup in March). On their way to Scottish Cup glory, Rangers beat Elgin City 4–1 in the first round at Ibrox, Motherwell 3–0 away in second round and Partick Thistle 3–0 at Ibrox in the quarter-finals. In the semi-final at Hampden Park, Rangers ran out comfortable 3–0 winners over East Fife.

Scottish FA Cup Final
23 APRIL 1949, HAMPDEN PARK, GLASGOW

Rangers (1) 4   v.   Clyde (1) 1
(Young (2) (both pens),   (Galletly)
Williamson, Duncanson)

Att. 108,435

Rangers: Bobby Brown, George Young, John "Tiger" Shaw, Ian McColl, Willie Woodburn, Sammy Cox, Willie Waddell, Jimmy Duncanson, Willie Thornton, Billy Williamson, Eddie Rutherford.

Did You Know That?
Rangers received a bye in the third round of the 1948–49 Scottish Cup, on their way to a 12th success in the competition.

❈ NEGRI ALMOST BECAME A THIEF ❈

In November 1997, Marco Negri's mother gave an interview to the *Sun* newspaper, during which she revealed that Marco had wanted to be a thief or a footballer when he was younger. When asked about the story Marco said: "It's true. Thank heaven I became a footballer." Marco only learned what his mother had said when Gazza told him that he was going to be taking his wallet out onto the pitch with him. Marco had no idea what Gazza was talking about, until the England midfielder showed him the paper.

❈ THE STAR OF DAVID SEEN AT IBROX ❈

During the 2004–05 season, Rangers fans were seen waving Israel's national flag, the Star of David, when Celtic were the visitors to Ibrox. The Rangers fans adopted the flag after they had seen a few Celtic fans parading Palestine's national flag at their games.

�֍ WIT AND WISDOM OF THE BLUES (8) ✷

"I spent the last ten minutes constantly asking the referee to blow for full time. I had nothing left."
John Greig, *on the 1972 European Cup-Winners' Cup final win*

✷ RANGERS IN EUROPE: 1967–68 TO 1977–78 ✷

Season	Comp.	Round	Opponents	Home	Away	Agg.
1967–68	FC	1st	Dynamo Dresden	2–1	1–1	3–2
		2nd	Cologne	3–0	1–3	4–3
		Qf	Leeds United	0–0	0–2	0–2
1968–69	FC	1st	Vojvodina	2–0	0–1	2–1
		2nd	Dundalk	6–1	3–0	9–1
		3rd	DWS Amsterdam	2–1	2–0	4–1
		Qf	Atletico Bilbao	4–1	0–2	4–3
		Sf	Newcastle United	0–0	0–2	0–2
1969–70	ECWC	1st	Steaua Bucharest	2–0	0–0	2–0
		2nd	Gornik	1–3	1–3	2–6
1970–71	FC	1st	Bayern Munich	1–1	0–1	1–2
1971–72	ECWC	1st	Rennes	1–0	1–1	2–1
		2nd	Sporting Lisbon	3–2	3–4	6–6
		(Rangers won on the away-goals rule)				
		Qf	Torino	1–0	1–1	2–1
		Sf	Bayern Munich	2–0	1–1	3–1
		F	Dynamo Moscow			3–2
		(Played at the Nou Camp, Barcelona)				
1972–73	SC		Ajax	1–3	2–3	3–6
		(Inaugural Super Cup. Rangers banned from defending Cup-Winners' Cup after crowd trouble at previous year's final)				
1973–74	ECWC	1st	Ankaragucu	4–0	2–2	6–2
		2nd	Borussia Moenchengladbach	0–3	3–2	3–5
1974–75			Rangers failed to qualify for Europe			
1975–76	ECWC	1st	Bohemians	4–1	1–1	5–2
		2nd	St Etienne	1–2	0–2	1–4
1976–77	EC	1st	FC Zurich	1–1	0–1	1–2
1977–78	ECWC	prelim	Young Boys Berne	1–0	2–2	3–2
		1st	Twente Enschede	0–0	0–3	0–3

Key: SC – European Super Cup; EC – European Cup; FC – Fairs' Cup; ECWC – European Cup-Winners' Cup

❋ SCOTTISH TEAMS' EUROPEAN RANKINGS ❋

For the 2005–06 season, the Scottish teams that participated in Europe were seeded for the various tournaments depending on each team's official UEFA ranking. UEFA's rankings are calculated by multiplying a third of UEFA's coefficient for the country by the total number of points gained by that team (two for a win and one for a draw) from the first round proper of each competition over the previous five years. The Scottish teams' rankings and points total used for the 2005–06 season were as follows:

Team	Points	Rank
Celtic	63.476	22
Rangers	40.476	48
Hibernian	12.476	158
Dundee United	10.476	179

❋ WHY THE "OLD FIRM"? ❋

The term "Old Firm" goes back over 100 years. At the beginning of the 20th century, there was a considerable amount of suspicion in Scottish football that Rangers and Celtic, despite their fierce rivalry on the pitch, would act together for their own benefit rather than for the benefit of Scottish football as a whole. Indeed, there was a famous cartoon in the *Scottish Referee* that used the phrase "The Old Firm" to describe Celtic and Rangers collectively. Even both sets of fans suspected that Celtic and Rangers would sometimes "stage" results to secure extra revenue. One of the main causes for the riot at the 1909 Scottish Cup final replay was the fans' belief that the clubs had colluded to arrange a second drawn game in order to reap the financial rewards of a third game (second replay).

❋ CROWD CAUSE REFEREE TO END PLAY ❋

In the Scottish Cup final replay at the West of Scotland Cricket Ground on 7 April 1877, the game between Rangers and Vale of Leven ended in a 1–1 draw after extra time. However, the full 30 minutes of extra time was never played, as Rangers claimed that a shot from Willie Dunlop had crossed the line, struck a fan and rebounded into the hands of the Vale of Leven goalkeeper. Referee James Kerr ruled against Rangers, which provoked the crowd to encroach on to the field and he had no option but to call an end to the game. Rangers lost the second replay, at First Hampden Park, 3–2.

❋ RANGERS XI OF THE 1940s ❋

1
Bobby
BROWN

2
Sammy
COX

3
Jock
SHAW

4
Ian
McCOLL

5
Willie
WOODBURN

6
Scot
SYMON

7
Willie
WADDELL

8
Torry
GILLICK

9
Willie
THORNTON

10
Jimmy
DUNCANSON

11
Jimmy
CASKIE

Reserves
Douglas *GRAY* • Billy *WILLIAMSON* • Bobby *BOLT*
Eddie *RUTHERFORD* • Willie *RAE*
Manager
Bill *STRUTH*

Did You Know That?

In season 1939–40, Rangers won two league championships. The Scottish First Division kicked off on 12 August 1939, but was suspended on 2 September after the onset of the Second World War. Rangers, with four wins and a draw from their five games, were crowned champions. From 21 October 1939, the Scottish Regional League Western Division was introduced, which Rangers also won. On 4 May 1940, they beat Dundee United 1–0 to add the Scottish Emergency War Cup.

❋ RANGERS OPPONENTS' DOUBLE AWAY TIE ❋

In the 1998–99 UEFA Cup, Rangers were drawn against the Republic of Ireland side Shelbourne, from Dublin, in the preliminary round. Rangers were orginally drawn at home in the first leg but UEFA decided that Shelbourne should play the first leg as the home side at Tranmere's Prenton Park, because of possible security risks posed by civil unrest in Northern Ireland; Rangers won 5–3 "away" and 2–0 at Ibrox.

❋ McCOIST PLAYS FOR CELTIC ❋

In 2000, the movie *A Shot at Glory* was made. In the movie Ally McCoist[†] plays a former Celtic player, Jackie McQuillan, and footage of the movie shows McCoist in his Ibrox glory days with a Celtic shirt superimposed over his Rangers shirt. Celtic's Didier Agathe played for Rangers in the movie.

❋ THE SCOTTISH FIRST DIVISION ❋

The Scottish First Division was established in 1890. The Scottish Football Association remained adamant that football was a game for amateurs, even though some clubs were paying players behind the SFA's back. When St Bernard's were suspended by the Scottish FA for paying one of their players, the club reformed under a new name, with Renton providing their first opposition in a friendly game. The SFA then expelled Renton from the League in its opening season and their playing record was expunged from the record books. Scotland's leading football club at the time, Queen's Park, declined to join the League, stating that they did not wish to be associated with an organization that had been tainted with illegal professionalism. At the end of the first ever Scottish First Division season, Rangers finished level on points with Dumbarton and, as goal difference was not a rule at the time, a play-off was arranged – it ended 2–2 and the trophy was shared.

❋ GREIG THE HERO ❋

John Greig captained Scotland to one of their most memorable international victories. On 15 April 1967 Scotland beat reigning world champions England 3–2 at Wembley in a 1968 European Championships qualifying game. Greig saved what looked like a certain goal for England when he headed a clearance off the line.

❋ THREE MICHELIN STARS ❋

Former Rangers player, now celebrity chef, Gordon Ramsey, was the first Scot to receive a coveted Michelin star when his restaurant "Gordon Ramsey at Hospital Road, Chelsea" won three in 2001.

[†]*During filming, Ally McCoist wanted Rangers to win the match at the end of the movie, and when the producer changed the script, the teams were also changed around, making McCoist's part in the movie that of a former Celtic player ... something that he wasn't too happy about.*

❈ SUPER SWEDE SCORES TWO CORNERS ❈

In the 1967–68 season, Rangers' Swedish winger Orjan Persson[†] scored two goals, both from corner-kicks, in Rangers' 5–0 thrashing of Stirling Albion at Ibrox.

❈ THE BIGOT ❈

During the 1970s, James Barclay wrote a play called *The Bigot*[††], a comedy that is reflective of modern day life in Glasgow. The play tells the story of a Rangers fanatic, Andra Thomson, and his long-suffering wife, Annie, their children and their friends. Andra's world has two spheres: alcohol and football. The play follows Andra in the lead-up to his team's Scottish Cup final encounter against Celtic, but his life undergoes a dramatic change prior to the big game. First of all, his daughter informs him that she is going to marry a Jewish boy called Clarence; and then his son Peter elects to join the priesthood. To top things off, Rangers can only manage a draw with their Old Firm rivals. The play is about Glaswegians laughing at themselves from the inside out and was a huge success; it was quickly followed by *Still a Bigot* and *Always a Bigot*.

❈ BLUES BEAT THE BLUES ❈

Lev.ki Sofia, nicknamed "The Blues", eliminated Rangers in the first round of the 1993–94 European Cup on the away-goals rule.

❈ SAINTS SPOIL IBROX PARTY ❈

In the summer of 1976, Rangers hosted a pre-season tournament at Ibrox. In the final, Southampton, the underdogs who had defeated the mighty Manchester United in the 1976 English FA Cup final at Wembley, beat the hosts 2–1.

❈ BLUES SET BLUES' RECORD HOME CROWD ❈

In 1948, the record home attendance for Stair Park was set when Rangers played Stranraer there in front of 6,500 fans. Stranraer are nicknamed "The Blues".

[†]*Orjan Persson and Lennart Wing were the first internationals to play for Dundee United.*
[††]*A number of Rangers fans complained that publicity material issued by The Pavilion Theatre in Glasgow for the play was "bigoted".*

❋ RANGERS' MILITARY MEDAL HERO ❋

James Hamilton Speirs, the fifth of six children, was born in the Govanhill area of Glasgow in 1886. In 1905, he joined Maryhill FC and, after just a few games, he was signed by Rangers at the end of the 1904–05 season, aged just 19. Over the following three years, he played a total of 62 Scottish League and Cup games, and scored 29 goals for the 'Gers before being transferred to Clyde in 1908 (scoring ten goals in 20 Scottish First Division and Scottish Cup games for "The Bully Wee"). In March 1908, Jimmy won his only international cap for Scotland, in the Home Championship game against Wales in Dundee.

In July 1909 he signed for Bradford City and was appointed the team captain. Jimmy played in 86 league games – scoring 29 times – and ten FA Cup games – scoring four goals – for "The Bantams". In 1911, he scored for Bradford City after just 15 minutes of their FA Cup final replay at Old Trafford to help the Yorkshire side lift the cup.

In December 1912, Jimmy was brought to Leeds City FC by the legendary Herbert Chapman, who would later manage both Huddersfield Town and Arsenal to English League championship success. At the time, the reported fee of £1,400 was enormous, as the average weekly wage was just £2, while the top players in England were earning just £4 per week. In total, Jimmy played 73 league games for the Elland Road club, scoring 32 goals, plus a further five FA Cup games.

During the 1914–15 season, Jimmy played his last match in Leeds City's final league game of the season and, despite being married with two young children, he returned to Glasgow and volunteered to enlist in the Cameron Highlanders. He was immediately posted to a reserve battalion at Inverness. In March 1916, Corporal Jimmy Speirs was posted to France. In May 1917, Corporal Speirs won the Military Medal for bravery in the field and was promoted to the rank of sergeant. Tragically, at the age of just 31, Jimmy was reported wounded and missing in action on 10 August 1917, during the famous Battle of Passchendaele (the Third Battle of Ypres). Jimmy's wife was eventually informed that Sergeant Jimmy Speirs had died on, or shortly after, going missing in action.

Speaking after his death, Lieutenant-Colonel (Rtd) A.M. Cumming, OBE, of the Highlanders' Regimental Museum, Inverness, described Jimmy as: "A remarkable man ... to have played for Scotland, won the FA Cup, scored the winning goal and won a Military Medal is remarkable by any standards."

✳ YOUNG TO THE DOUBLE RESCUE ✳

In the 1952–53 season, Rangers completed the Double, but it was a close call. In the Scottish Cup final, the Rangers goalkeeper, George Niven, had to leave the field because of an injury after just 18 minutes. Centre-half George Young donned the goalkeeper's jersey and played well enough between the posts to earn Rangers a 1–1 draw with Aberdeen. Rangers now needed just three points from their last two league games to clinch both the championship and the Double. Three days after lifting the cup, Rangers beat Dundee 3–1 and now needed only a point against Queen of the South. Trailing 1–0 to Queen of the South, Willie Waddell scored Rangers' equalizer to earn the draw – it was good enough to secure the championship and the Double. Rangers' 75-year-old manager, Bill Struth, had just won his 18th championship and tenth Scottish Cup in charge of the club – a record unequalled in British football. He also won three Scottish League Cups, making it a total haul of 31 domestic trophies.

✳ RANGERS BEATEN BY THE ARABS ✳

Dundee United, nicknamed "The Terrors", but commonly referred to as "The Arabs", beat Rangers 1–0 in the 1994 Scottish Cup final. It was the first time in their history that they had won the cup – they had lost their six previous finals.

✳ SOUNESS FALLS FOUL OF FANS ✳

Graeme Souness underwent major heart surgery in April 1992, but an interview he gave from his hospital bed proved a major turning point in his career. Souness gave an exclusive interview with the *Sun* newspaper on the anniversary of the Hillsborough disaster – a paper that Liverpool fans had boycotted after it had printed unsubstantiated stories about Liverpool fans' actions on that fateful day, 15 April 1989. Many fans turned against Souness after this and, in January 1994, after a humiliating FA Cup exit to Bristol City, Souness and Liverpool parted company.

✳ NO WAY PAST ✳

During the 1992–93 season Rangers enjoyed a remarkable run of 44 games unbeaten. Andy Goram was between the posts in all 44 games and conceded just 30 goals; he only conceded 18 goals in 34 league games.

❋ UP FOR THE CUP (7) ❋

On 29 April 1953, Rangers beat Aberdeen 1–0 in the Scottish Cup final replay at Hampden Park just four days after the two sides had played out a 1–1 draw at the same venue. The cup success made up for Rangers' semi-final exit to Kilmarnock in the Scottish League Cup earlier in the season. On their way to Hampden success in 1953, Rangers beat Arbroath 4–0 in the first round at Ibrox, Dundee 2–0 away in the second round, Morton 3–1 away in the third round, Celtic 2–0 at Ibrox in the quarter-finals and Hearts 2–1 at Hampden Park in the semi-finals.

SCOTTISH FA CUP FINAL (REPLAY)
29 APRIL 1953, HAMPDEN PARK, GLASGOW
Rangers (1) 1   v.   Aberdeen (0) 0
(Prentice)
Att. 129,761
Rangers: George Niven, George Young, John Little, Ian McColl, Willie Woodburn, Willie Pryde, Willie Waddell, Derek Grierson, Billie Simpson, Willie Paton, Johnny Hubbard.

❋ A CHANGE OF COLOURS ❋

Lifelong Rangers fan, Graeme Dott, the winner of the 2006 World Professional Snooker Championship, brought the trophy to Ibrox to show off to the fans prior to Rangers' 2–0 home win over Heart of Midlothian on 7 May 2006. However, Graeme had to ask the sponsors of the World Professional Snooker Championship, 888.com, to make a special set of blue ribbons for the trophy. The sponsors' traditional colours are green and Graeme didn't want to take the trophy onto the pitch at Ibrox with green ribbons attached to it.

❋ RANGERS BOOED OFF PITCH ❋

On 27 April 1968, Rangers lost 3–2 to Aberdeen at Ibrox in the Scottish First Division. Going into the game, Rangers had been unbeaten in the league with 61 points from a possible 66, but Aberdeen's last-minute winner meant that they had handed the championship to Celtic – who had to lose 16–0 at Dunfermline Athletic for Rangers to have won the title on goal difference! The mathematical improbability remained just that, as Celtic won the game 2–1. Following the defeat, Rangers players were booed off the pitch.

❊ WIT AND WISDOM OF THE BLUES (9) ❊

"I have told Graeme he has made the biggest mistake of his life."
David Murray, on Graeme Souness leaving for Liverpool in 1991

❊ HAVE YOU SEEN THE GLASGOW RANGERS ❊

Have you seen the Glasgow Rangers
Have you seen the boys in blue
They're admired by all who know them
If you knew them so would you
Oh they have played away in Monaco
They have played in the USA
But the greatest game in history
Is the game on New Year's Day
For it's the home of famous heroes
And their praises have been sung
Willie Waddell, Torry Gillick
Alan Morton and George Young
And when all my life has ended
And when death has made its mark
Will you scatter all my ashes
On the slopes of Ibrox Park
And with the Angels I'll be singing
Up in heaven there up above
I'll be singing Follow Follow
To the Rangers that I love
And with my flute I will be playing
In the valleys and the glens
I'll be happy and contented
When the Rangers win again

❊ NO WORLD CUP PLACE FOR BLUES ❊

On 15 April 1950, Scotland played England at Hampden Park in a World Cup qualifying and Home Championship game. Scotland lost 1–0, but still qualified for the finals after finishing as the group's runner-up. However, the SFA declared that if the side was not good enough to be crowned British champions then they would not go to the finals. After the game, the England captain, Billy Wright, pleaded with his opposite number, Rangers' George Young, to ask the SFA to change their mind, but the SFA refused to give in. Four other Rangers players also played in the game.

✳ JOHN GREIG ✳

John Greig was born in Edinburgh on 11 September 1942. He made his Rangers bow in September 1961 in a 4–1 League Cup win over Airdrie; playing at inside-right, he marked his debut with a goal. During the 1961–62 season, he played 11 times for the club as a centre-forward and scored seven goals. However, it was the 1962–63 season that really launched his Rangers career, as this was the season in which he earned a regular place in the starting line-up. On New Year's Day 1963, John scored his first Old Firm goal in a 4–0 trouncing of Celtic.

By the end of the 1962–63 season, Greig had already been switched to right-half, where he linked up superbly with Jim Baxter, and collected the first of his five Scottish League championship-winners' medals (1962–63, 1963–64, 1974–75, 1975–76 and 1977–78). He rounded off the season in style by collecting a Scottish Cup-winners' medal in Rangers' first Cup final victory over Celtic in 35 years. Despite his youth, Greig was not out of place in a Rangers team comprising such legends as Jim Baxter, Ralph Brand and Willie Henderson.

In the 1963–64 season, Greig was an integral part of the Rangers team that won the Treble: they won the championship with a six-point margin over Kilmarnock, the League Cup, with a comprehensive 5–0 drubbing of Morton, and the Scottish Cup with a 3–1 victory over Dundee United. Unbelievably, Greig played in every match for Rangers in all three of the domestic competitions. On 11 April 1964, he won his first international cap for Scotland in a 1–0 win over England at Hampden Park and went on to collect a further 43 caps for his country, captaining the side on many occasions. His proudest moment in international football came on 9 November 1965, when he scored the only goal of the game in Scotland's 1–0 win over Italy at Hampden Park.

John won his second League Cup-winners' medal in 1964–65 and, around this time, Greig was approached by English League clubs, but he remained loyal to Rangers; this loyalty is reflected in the fact that he holds the record for the most Rangers league appearances with 496 and is second only to Dougie Gray (1925–47) for the most Rangers appearances (in all competitions) with an astonishing 857. He scored 120 goals for Rangers and captained the side to their only European succcess, the 1972 European Cup-Winners' Cup. In addition to his five championship-winners' medals, John also won six Scottish Cups and four League Cups. His place in Rangers history was guaranteed in 1999, when he was voted Rangers' greatest ever player by the fans.

Did You Know That?
John Greig managed Rangers from 1978 to 1983.

※ IS THERE ANYBODY OUT THERE? ※

The Old Firm game between Celtic and Rangers at Celtic Park, on Sunday, 2 May 1999, was the subject of a test. The Scottish Premier League were planning for a worldwide pay-per-listen scheme of SPL games via the Internet, despite the fact that BBC Radio 5 Live's commentary of the Old Firm clash was available free of charge. However, SPL's director of marketing, Paul Blanchard, said: "We will be putting the commentary of Celtic and Rangers on our website this Sunday evening and are testing it with a view to moving into the pay-per-listen market. We don't view ourselves as in competition with domestic broadcasters, as this is basically for an overseas audience." Rangers won the game 3–0 to claim their first ever championship-clinching victory at Celtic Park.

※ ONE OF FOUR ※

Rangers are just one of four Scottish clubs to have won a European tie on the away-goals rule:

UEFA Cup, third round, 2002–03
Celtic v. Celta Vigo (ESP), 1–0 and 1–2
(Celtic win on the away-goals rule)
UEFA Cup, first qualifying round, 2002–03
FC Vaduz (LIE) v. Livingston, 1–1 and 0–0
(Livingston win on the away-goals rule)
European Cup, quarter-final, 1983–84
SK Rapid Vienna (AUT) v. Dundee United, 2–1 and 0–1
(Dundee United win on the away-goals rule)
UEFA Cup, first round, 1979–80
Dundee United v. RSC Anderlecht (BEL), 0–0 and 1–1
(Dundee United win on the away-goals rule)
European Cup-Winners' Cup, second round, 1971–72
Rangers v. Sporting Lisbon (POR), 3–2 and 3–4 (aet)
(Rangers win on the away-goals rule)

※ A STAR IS BORN ※

When the club went on a pre-season tour of Russia in the summer of 1962, John Greig impressed the Rangers management team with some outstanding performances at wing-half in place of Jim Baxter, who was not on tour. His place in the side was assured from that moment on.

✳ WE ARE THE CHAMPIONS (7) ✳

In the 1956–57 season, Rangers retained the Scottish First Division championship for the first time in seven years. However, although Rangers' league form was good throughout the season, their cup form was poor. First Celtic helped put them out of the League Cup with a 0–0 draw at Ibrox in a group game, and then Celtic knocked them out of the Scottish Cup. It was Hearts who set the early pace in the league, and for much of the season Rangers were playing catch-up. However, a superb, 16-match unbeaten run – from 12 January 1957 to the end of the season – saw Rangers clinch the Scottish First Division title by two points from Hearts.

Scottish League Division One
1956–57

		P	W	D	L	F	A	W	D	L	F	A	Pts
1.	Rangers	34	13	2	2	48	22	13	1	3	48	26	55
2.	Heart of Midlothian	34	11	3	3	40	23	13	2	2	41	25	53
3.	Kilmarnock	34	9	6	2	35	20	7	4	6	22	19	42
4.	Raith Rovers	34	10	2	5	52	32	6	5	6	32	26	39
5.	Celtic	34	9	6	2	33	14	6	2	9	25	29	38
6.	Aberdeen	34	10	1	6	36	24	8	1	8	43	35	38
7.	Motherwell	34	9	2	6	41	32	7	3	7	31	34	37
8.	Partick Thistle	34	11	3	3	37	18	2	5	10	16	33	34
9.	Hibernian	34	6	8	3	38	20	6	1	10	31	36	33
10.	Dundee	34	10	2	5	38	23	3	4	10	17	38	32
11.	Airdrieonians	34	8	2	7	45	40	5	2	10	32	49	30
12.	St Mirren	34	8	3	6	37	25	4	3	10	21	47	30
13.	Queen's Park	34	9	2	6	33	19	2	5	10	22	40	29
14.	Falkirk	34	5	2	10	28	35	5	6	6	23	35	28
15.	East Fife	34	7	3	7	33	34	3	3	11	26	48	26
16.	Queen of the South	34	8	3	6	35	37	2	2	13	19	59	25
17.	Dunfermline Athletic	34	6	3	8	31	36	3	3	11	23	38	24
18.	Ayr United	34	5	2	10	27	35	2	3	12	21	54	19

✳ McLEISH LOSES LAST HOME OLD FIRM GAME ✳

Rangers lost 1–0 to Celtic at Ibrox on 12 February 2006, in what was Alex McLeish's last home Old Firm game as Rangers' manager. The defeat left Rangers 21 points behind Celtic and eight behind Hearts. They ended the season a point behind Hearts, but 18 adrift of Celtic.

❋ RANGERS IN EUROPE: 1978–79 TO 1988–89 ❋

Season	*Comp.*	*Round*	*Opponents*	*Home*	*Away*	*Agg.*
1978–79	EC	1st	Juventus	2–0	0–1	2–1
		2nd	PSV Eindhoven	0–0	3–2	3–2
		3rd	Cologne	1–1	0–1	1–2
1979–80	ECWC	prelim	Lilliestrom Fortuna	1–0	2–0	3–0
		1st	Dusseldorf	2–1	0–0	2–1
		2nd	Valencia	1–3	1–1	2–4
1980–81		Rangers failed to qualify for Europe				
1981–82	ECWC	1st	Dukla Prague	2–1	0–3	2–4
1982–83	UEFA	1st	Borussia Dortmund	2–0	0–0	2–0
		2nd	Cologne	2–1	0–5	2–6
1983–84	ECWC	1st	Valetta	10–0	8–0	18–0
		(Scottish record in Europe)				
		2nd	FC Porto	2–1	0–1	2–2
		(FC Porto won on the away-goals rule)				
1984–85	UEFA	1st	Bohemians	2–0	2–3	4–3
		2nd	Inter Milan	3–1	0–3	3–4
1985–86	UEFA	1st	Atletico Osasuna	1–0	0–2	1–2
1986–87	UEFA	1st	Ilves Tampere	4–0	0–2	4–2
		2nd	Boavista	2–1	1–0	3–1
		3rd	Borussia Moenchengladbach	1–1	0–0	1–1
		(Borussia Moenchengladbach won on the away-goals rule)				
1987–88	EC	1st	Dynamo Kiev	2–0	0–1	2–1
		2nd	Gornik Zabrze	3–1	1–1	4–2
		3rd	Steaua Bucharest	2–1	0–2	2–3

Key: EC – European Cup; UEFA – UEFA Cup; ECWC – European Cup-Winners' Cup

❋ SIGNED FOR FREE TWICE ❋

In May 1973, Rangers signed Johnnie Hamilton† on a free transfer from Hibs. Hamilton spent five seasons at Ibrox before being released on another free transfer in the summer of 1978. He played 77 times for Rangers (59 league, 11 cup, six League Cup and once in Europe) and scored eight goals (five league, two cup, one League Cup).

†Hamilton made his Rangers debut coming on as a substitute at Parkhead in a 1–0 league loss to Celtic in January 1974. His final appearance for Rangers was also as a substitute, in a 2–0 league win at Clydebank in April 1978. Despite making less than 80 appearances for the club, he won both league championship- and Scottish Cup-winners' medals in 1976 and 1978: he completed his domestic medal treble with a League Cup-winners' medal.

❊ RANGERS XI OF THE 1950s ❊

1
George
NIVEN

2
George
YOUNG

3
John
LITTLE

4
Ian
McCOLL

5
Willie
WOODBURN

6
Willie
PRYDE

7
Willie
WADDELL

8
Derek
GRIERSON

9
Billie
SIMPSON

10
Willie
PATON

11
Johnny
HUBBARD

Reserves
Norrie *MARTIN* • Sammy *COX* • Willie *TELFER*,
Alex *SCOTT* • Sammy *BAIRD*
Manager
Scot *SYMON*

Did You Know That?

At the end of the 1953–54 season, Rangers embarked on a nine-match tour of the USA. They won seven, drew one and lost one of the games (both to Chelsea). Chelsea went on to win the English First Division championship the following season for the first time in their history, a feat they would not achieve again until the 2004–05 season. On 15 June 1954, Bill Struth stepped down after 34 years in charge of the club.

❊ WIT AND WISDOM OF THE BLUES (10) ❊

"Rangers are a big club and I want to win things. They will help me do that."
***Mo Johnston**, explaining why he joined Rangers from Nantes in 1989*

❊ RANGERS BEAT CUP HOODOO ❊

In 1928, Rangers beat Celtic 4–0 in the Scottish Cup final to claim the trophy for the first time since 1903.

❋ AMORUSO BANNED FOR SPITTING ❋

On 18 March 2003, Lorenzo Amoruso was handed a four-match ban after being found guilty of deliberately spitting on Ayr United's striker James Grady. The incident took place during the Scottish Cup tie at Somerset Park on 22 February. Amoruso insisted that he did not intentionally spit at Grady, but BBC television cameras captured the incident and a Scottish Football Association review panel decided that Amoruso had a case to answer. The SFA disciplinary committee handed out a two-match ban and also added 12 points to Amoruso's disciplinary record, which resulted in a further two-game suspension.

❋ SIXTH TIME LUCKY ❋

In 1894, Rangers finally lifted the Scottish FA Cup having lost all five of the previous finals they had appeared in.

❋ SCOTTISH CHAMPIONS FROM 1891–2006 ❋

There have been 110 Scottish championships between 1891 and 2006. Here is a breakdown by the most won:

51	Rangers††
40	Celtic
4	Heart of Midlothian, Hibernian, Aberdeen
2	Dumbarton††
1	Third Lanark, Motherwell†, Dundee, Kilmarnock, Dundee United

❋ A GAME THAT HAD TO BE MISSED ❋

During the 1976–77 season, Davie Cooper, then at Clydebank, made his debut for Scotland Under-21s. Scotland played Czechoslovakia in Pilsen in a game that ended 0–0. Alongside him in the Scottish side were Roy Aitken, George Burley and John Wark. His first cap that bitterly cold October night meant that he missed Clydebank's game – the only match he missed all season for "The Bankies".

†*Between 1905 and the outbreak of the Second World War in 1939, only Motherwell, in 1932, were able to break the Old Firm domination of in the Scottish League. Had Rangers triumphed in 1932, it would have been their sixth consecutive title and, after winning the championship again in 1933, 1934 and 1935, Rangers narrowly missed out on setting a record of nine championships in a row, a feat Celtic achieved 39 years later.*

††*Rangers and Dumbarton shared the 1891 Scottish championship, drawing a playoff game 2–2.*

❋ LIKE FATHER, LIKE SON ❋

Mark Hateley's father, Tony, was also a professional footballer and centre-forward who played for a number of clubs during his career, including Aston Villa and Liverpool.

❋ MILLER JOINS CELTIC ❋

On 19 January 2006, former Rangers player Kenny Miller joined Celtic. Only two post-war players have played in an Old Firm derby for both sides, Alfie Conn and Mo Johnston.

❋ FOUR POINTS DROPPED ❋

In the 1899–1900 season, Rangers ran away with the Scottish League championship, dropping just four points along the way, three of them to Celtic.

❋ COLIN STEIN ❋

Colin Stein was born on 10 May 1947 and was a star player for Rangers during the 1960s and '70s. He also played for Coventry City.

❋ GAZZA THE PRANKSTER (3) ❋

1. On his first night in Rome after signing for Lazio, he gave his minder the slip and placed his shoes by an open window in his bedroom and then hid in a wardrobe. The poor minder thought that Gazza had jumped to his death out of the window.
2. He once completely shredded his England team-mate Dennis Wise's Armani suit. When asked why he did it, he replied: "For a laugh."
3. He once took a television documentary crew to a beautiful Scottish cottage and informed the director that he had bought it. He then pretended he'd forgotten his key and knocked on the door. An old lady appeared and Gazza told her that he was filming an advertisement for soap powder and wanted to know whether she preferred Daz or Omo.
4. He taught every one of his Lazio team-mates to swear in English with a Geordie accent.
5. After paying for his ex-wife Sheryl's breast implants, he sent her a bunch of flowers to the hospital following her operation and addressed the card to "Dolly Parton".

❋ OLD FIRM'S CUP FINAL CONSISTENCY ❋

During the 20th century, 1991 was the only year ending in "1" where neither of the Old Firm teams took part in the Scottish Cup final.

1901	Hearts 4–3 Celtic	
1911	Celtic 2–0 Hamilton Academical	*(replay)*
1921	Partick Thistle 1–0 Rangers	
1931	Celtic 4–2 Motherwell	*(replay)*
1941	*Not held due to WWII*	
1951	Celtic 1–0 Motherwell	
1961	Dunfermline 2–0 Celtic	*(replay)*
1971	Celtic 2–1 Rangers	*(replay)*
1981	Rangers 4–1 Dundee United	*(replay)*
1991	Motherwell 4–3 Dundee United	*(aet)*

❋ McLEISH TO LEAVE ❋

On 9 February 2006, just five days after their humiliating 3–0 Scottish Cup loss to Hibernian at Ibrox, Alex McLeish announced that he would step down as the Rangers manager in the summer. Following the announcement, Rangers were automatically linked with the ex-manager of Lyon, Paul Le Guen†, who was eventually confirmed as McLeish's replacement.

❋ ALL-ROUND SCORERS ❋

During the 1912–13 season, Rangers beat Morton 3–0 away. Morton created quite a curious record during the course of that season, when every player who played for them scored at least one goal, including their goalkeeper who scored a penalty.

❋ A TEAM OF "Os" ❋

Including players from the 2005–06 season, 13 players whose surname ends with the letter "o" have played for the club: Amato, Amoruso, Andre Flo, Falco, Gattuso, Kelso, Mikhailichenko, Munro (Iain and Stuart), Novo, Prso, Riccio and Salenko. Sadly they would not have been able to form a team, as none of them was a goalkeeper!

†Le Guen was enjoying a sabbatical from football when he was linked with the Rangers job after having guided Lyon to three of their four successive French championships.

❋ BAXTER'S BRIDGE ❋

In 2005, the London Development Agency and Radio 5 Live asked fans to contact them and suggest a name for the footbridge at the new Wembley Stadium. Many Scotland fans seized the opportunity to embarrass the English FA and suggested Jim Baxter's name. Their attempts, however, were unsuccessful as "Billy the White Horse" won the vote.

❋ TOP OF THE POPS ❋

In 1990, "Gazza Mania" was in full swing and Paul took full advantage of it, releasing a single with Lindisfarne entitled *Fog on the Tyne* which reached No.2 in the UK music charts.

❋ THE BLUE SEA OF IBROX ❋

Ian Durrant won 19 caps for Scotland, 11 of them while he was still a player with Rangers.

❋ COOPER'S TAKINGS ❋

Davie Cooper's boss at the printing factory where he worked asked Jack Steedman, the owner of Clydebank, to persuade the teenager to turn professional. It is said that Steedman turned up at Davie's house with the takings (£300) from the social club's fruit machine to lure Davie to Clydebank.

❋ THE OLD FIRM'S SCOTTISH CUP DYNASTY ❋

One of Celtic or Rangers have only ever failed to reach the Scottish Cup final on 34 occasions since the inaugural cup was held in 1874.

❋ LOS MERENGUES HAMMER 'GERS ❋

Real Madrid, nicknamed "Los Merengues" ("The Whites"), beat Rangers 1–0 at Ibrox and 6–0 at Estadio Santiago Bernabeu in the first round of the 1963–64 European Cup. Real Madrid were formed in 1902 and copied the kit worn by the famous English side, Corinthians.

❋ SERIE A BUDDIES ❋

Mark Hateley and Ray Wilkins played together for AC Milan.

❊ RANGERS IN EUROPE (1) ❊

In the 1960–61 season, Rangers reached the final of the inaugural European Cup-Winners' Cup. In the first round, Rangers beat Hungary's Ferencvaros 5–4 on aggregate and then had an 11–0 aggregate win over Borussia Moenchengladbach of West Germany in the quarter-finals. In the semi-finals, Rangers were drawn against the English FA Cup winners Wolverhampton Wanderers. Rangers beat Wolves 2–0 at Ibrox in their first-leg "British Cup final" tie and drew the second leg 1–1 at Molineux three weeks later. However, Rangers were no match for Italian side Fiorentina in the final, which was played over two legs. In the first leg at Ibrox, despite 80,000 fans cheering on the 'Gers, Fiorentina won 2–0. The second leg was played in Florence, ten days later, and Rangers slipped up again, this time 2–1, to lose 4–1 on aggregate.

EUROPEAN CUP-WINNERS' CUP FINAL 1961

FIRST LEG

17 MAY 1961, IBROX PARK, GLASGOW

Rangers (0) 0   v.   Fiorentina (1) 2
(Milani 2)

Att. 80,000

Rangers: Billy Ritchie, Bobby Shearer, Bill Paterson, Eric Caldow, Harry Davis, Jim Baxter, Alex Scott, Ian McMillan, Bobby Hume, Ralph Brand, Davie Wilson.
Fiorentina: Albertosi, Robotti, Castelletti, Gonfiantini, Orzan, Rimbaldo, Hamrin, Micheli, Da Costa, Milani, Petris.

SECOND LEG

27 MAY 1961, STADIO COMUNALE, FLORENCE

Fiorentina (1) 2   v.   Rangers (0) 1
(Milani, Hamrin)   (Scott)

Att. 50,000

Fiorentina: Albertosi, Robotti, Castelletti, Gonfiantini, Orzan, Rimbaldo, Hamrin, Micheli, Da Costa, Milani, Petris.
Rangers: Billy Ritchie, Bobby Shearer, Bill Paterson, Eric Caldow, Harry Davis, Jim Baxter, Alex Scott, Ian McMillan, Jimmy Millar, Ralph Brand, Davie Wilson.

Did You Know That?

In Rangers' 8–0 win over Borussia Moenchengladbach at Ibrox, Ralph Brand became the first player to score a European hat-trick for the club.

❋ WIT AND WISDOM OF THE BLUES (11) ❋

"If I have one regret in my career, it is that I didn't join Rangers a lot sooner."
Ray Wilkins

❋ NINE IN A ROW ❋

Season	Pos	P	W	D	L	F	A	Pts
1988–89	1st	36	26	4	6	62	26	56
1989–90	1st	36	20	11	5	48	19	51
1990–91	1st	36	24	7	5	62	23	55
1991–92	1st	44	33	6	5	101	31	72
1992–93	1st	44	33	7	4	97	35	73
1993–94	1st	44	22	14	8	74	41	58
1994–95	1st	36	20	9	7	60	35	69
1995–96	1st	36	27	6	3	85	25	87
1996–97	1st	36	25	5	6	85	33	80

❋ ONE PLAYER, TWO RANGERS ❋

Jim Forrest was born in Glasgow in 1944 and was a schoolboy international who joined Rangers straight from school in 1960. Rangers farmed the teenager out to Drumchapel Amateurs for a while before he returned to the club. Forrest was at Ibrox until March 1967 and played 163 times, notching up an incredible tally of 145 goals. In the 1964–65 season, he scored 57 goals, which is still a post-war Scottish record. During his time at Rangers, he won a league championship-winners' medal in 1964, a Scottish League Cup-winners' medal in 1964 and 1965 and a Scottish Cup-winners' medal in 1966. He played five times for Scotland. After Rangers, Forrest played for Preston North End, Aberdeen and Hong Kong Rangers. His cousin, Alex Willoughby, also played with him for Drumchapel Amateurs, Rangers, Aberdeen (where he won a Scottish Cup-winners' medal in 1970) and Hong Kong Rangers.

❋ ATTILA THE HUN ❋

During his Rangers career, Mark Hateley was nicknamed "Attila[†]" because he scared the living daylights out of opposing defenders.

[†] *Attila the Hun (AD406–453) was the last and most powerful king of the Huns. He reigned over Europe's largest empire from AD434 until his death.*

❋ WE ARE THE CHAMPIONS (8) ❋

The 1963–64 season was another glorious Treble-winning campaign for Rangers. In the Scottish League Cup final, Rangers beat a plucky Morton side from the Second Division 5–0, while the Scottish Cup was secured after a 3–1 win over Dundee at Hampden Park. In the league, Rangers were unbeaten in their opening 13 games, but nerves seemed to creep into the side towards the end of 1963. Kilmarnock were in the driving seat at the turn of the year, but Rangers put together a run of five successive wins to surge in front. It was a lead they maintained until the end of the season and Rangers won their third championship in four years and their sixth in nine seasons. It was their first Treble in 15 years.

Scottish League Division One
1963–64

		P	W	D	L	F	A	W	D	L	F	A	Pts
1.	Rangers	34	13	1	3	43	19	12	4	1	42	12	55
2.	Kilmarnock	34	14	2	1	50	15	8	3	6	27	25	49
3.	Celtic	34	13	3	1	61	16	6	6	5	28	18	47
4.	Heart of Midlothian	34	8	5	4	39	23	11	4	2	35	17	47
5.	Dunfermline Athletic	34	11	3	3	41	16	7	6	4	23	17	45
6.	Dundee	34	11	3	3	53	27	9	2	6	41	23	45
7.	Partick Thistle	34	11	3	3	30	16	4	2	11	25	38	35
8.	Dundee United	34	10	2	5	43	23	3	6	8	22	26	34
9.	Aberdeen	34	5	5	7	26	26	7	3	7	27	27	32
10.	Hibernian	34	9	4	4	33	22	3	2	12	26	44	30
11.	Motherwell	34	7	5	5	29	23	2	6	9	22	39	29
12.	St Mirren	34	9	4	4	24	23	3	1	13	20	51	29
13.	St Johnstone	34	6	2	8	27	32	5	3	9	27	38	28
14.	Falkirk	34	7	4	6	24	26	4	2	11	30	58	28
15.	Airdrieonians	34	7	3	7	34	41	4	1	12	18	56	26
16.	Third Lanark	34	5	3	9	27	36	4	4	9	20	38	25
17.	Queen of the South	34	3	3	11	23	47	2	3	12	17	45	16
18.	East Stirlingshire	34	4	2	11	19	36	1	0	16	18	55	12

❋ RECORD FRIENDLY ATTENDANCE ❋

On 17 October 1961, a record crowd for a friendly match – 104,493 – saw Rangers draw 2–2 with Eintracht Frankfurt at Hampden Park. Eintracht lost the 1960 European Cup final, also at Hampden.

❊ RANGERS IN EUROPE: 1988–89 TO 1997–98 ❊

Season	Comp.	Round	Opponents	Home	Away	Agg.
1988–89	UEFA	1st	Katowice	1–0	4–2	5–2
		2nd	Cologne	1–1	0–2	1–3
1989–90	EC	1st	Bayern Munich	1–3	0–0	1–3
1990–91	EC	1st	Valetta	6–0	4–0	10–0
		2nd	Red Star Belgrade	1–1	0–3	1–4
1991–92	EC	1st	Sparta Prague	2–1	0–1	2–2
		(Sparta Prague won on the away-goals rule)				
1992–93	EC	1st	Lyngby	2–0	1–0	3–0
		2nd	Leeds United	2–1	2–1	4–2
		GS	Marseille	2–2	2–2	
		GS	Club Brugge	2–1	1–1	
		GS	CSKA Moscow	0–0	0–1	
1993–94	EC	1st	Lev.ki Sofia	3–2	1–2	4–4
		(Lev.ki Sofia won on the away-goals rule)				
1994–95	EC	1st	AEK Athens	0–1	0–2	0–3
1995–96	EC	1st	A. Famagusta	1–0	0–0	1–0
		GS	Steaua Bucharest	1–1	0–1	
		GS	Borussia Dortmund	2–2	2–2	
		GS	Juventus	0–4	1–4	
1996–97	EC	1st	Alania Vladlkavkaz	3–1	7–2	10–3
		Gs	Grasshoppers	2–1	0–3	
		Gs	Auxerre	1–2	1–2	
		Gs	Ajax	0–1	1–4	
1997–98	EC	pre 1	GI Gotu	5–0	6–0	11–0
		pre 2	IFK Gothenburg	0–3	1–1	1–4
		(Failed to qualify for Champions League.				
		Entered into UEFA Cup)				
	UEFA	1st	RC Strasbourg	1–2	1–2	2–4

Key: EC – European Cup/Champions League (GS = Group Stage); UEFA – UEFA Cup

❊ THIRD MANAGER IN 65 YEARS ❊

An incredible 65 years after the club appointed its first ever manager, Scot Symon[†] became the third man to take charge of the club when he was made manager in 1954. The new manager simply took over where Bill Struth had left off by bringing trophy after trophy to Ibrox. Symon won six league championships, five Scottish Cups and four League Cups.

[†]*In 1963–64, Scot Symon led Rangers to the domestic Treble, becoming only the second manager in Scottish football to do so – the other being Struth.*

❊ RANGERS GOALKEEPER HUMILIATED ❊

Stewart Kennedy of Rangers was between the posts for Scotland when England hammered five goals past him at Wembley on 24 May 1975[†]. His Rangers team-mates Sandy Jardine and Derek Parlane also played in the game.

❊ SLIM JIM'S SNAP, CRACKLE AND POP ❊

On Saturday, 4 March 1967, Jim Baxter played for Sunderland in their 3–0 win over their fiercest rivals, Newcastle United, in front of 50,000 ecstatic Sunderland fans at Roker Park. Slim Jim was mesmerizing in the game and tortured the Magpies' defence. In the following Monday's edition of the *Northern Echo*, Frank Johnson wrote about how Baxter took the mickey out of Newcastle: "This kid looks like being Sunderland's best outside-right since the days of Harry Hooper. He has the heart of a lion and a snap-crackle-and-pop brain."

❊ A RECORD POINTS TALLY ❊

The Scottish First Division was expanded for the 1919–20 season and, in the course of clinching the title, Rangers set a new record points total of 71 and scored 106 goals in their 42 league games.

❊ THE WEE BLUE DEVIL ❊

Alex Morton, nicknamed "The Wee Blue Devil", helped Rangers to seven Scottish championships during the 1920s and two more in the 1930s. Despite standing only 5ft 4in high, Morton terrorized defences with his mesmerizing dribbling ability, speed and close ball control.

❊ BOWLED OUT ❊

Representing Scotland, Andy Goram dismissed the England Test cricketer Richard Blakey in a NatWest Trophy game against Yorkshire in 1989. The Rangers legend was a talented league cricketer who appeared for various clubs, including Delph and Dobcross, Moorside and East Lancashire Paper Mills in the Saddleworth League.

[†]*The 5–1 defeat ended a run of seven unbeaten away matches for Scotland (two wins and five draws), which included three games at the 1974 World Cup finals.*

❈ ANDY GORAM ❈

Andrew Lewis Goram was born on 13 April 1964 in Bury, England. He began his proferssional career at Oldham Athletic, where he served the club for seven years. In October 1987, he moved to Hibernian and spent four seasons at Easter Road playing 138 league games for the Hi-Bees. Prior to joing Hibs, Andy had already been capped by Scotland during his time with Oldham Athletic, despite the fact that he had been born in England. During his time at Hibs he became a dual international, representing Scotland at both football and cricket.

In June 1991, Walter Smith splashed out £1 million to bring Andy to Ibrox as a direct replacement for Chris Woods. Andy made his Rangers debut in a 6–0 home thrashing against St Johnstone on 10 August 1991 and, during the 1991–92 season, he played in all 55 of Rangers' competitive fixtures, winning a Scottish League championship-winners' medal and a Scottish Cup-winners' medal after Rangers' 2–1 victory over Airdrie in the final. Things got even better for Andy in the 1992–93 season, as Rangers clinched the Treble (with victories over Aberdeen in both cup finals), while Andy also starred for Rangers in their Champions League campaign as they came within one game of reaching the final. He played in all ten European games – including the "Battle of Britain" victory over Leeds United – and conceded just seven goals as Rangers went through the competition unbeaten. Andy won both the Scottish PFA Player of the Year and the Scottish Football Writers' Player of the Year that season.

In the 1993–94 season, Andy won the Scottish League championship and Scottish League Cup with a victory over his old club, Hibernian, in the final. However, in December 1994, he suffered a serious knee injury which ruled him out for the remaining games of the season and which would trouble him for the rest of his career. He returned to win the Double with Rangers in 1995–96 and was then part of the Rangers team that clinched the "nine in a row" the following season. Andy played his 260th and last game for the club in the 1998 1–2 Scottish Cup final defeat by Hearts, before he packed his bags and joined Motherwell. Later in his career, he had spells with Notts County, Sheffield United, Manchester United, Coventry City, Queen of the South and Elgin City.

During his time with Glasgow Rangers, Andy won five Scottish League championships, three Scottish Cups, two Scottish League Cups and 20 of his 48 Scotland caps. Between the posts, he kept an incredible 107 clean sheets for the club and, in 2001, he received the ultimate accolade from the Rangers fans when they voted him Rangers' greatest ever goalkeeper in a poll.

✳ IBROX HOSTS SCOTTISH FA CUP FINAL ✳

Ibrox Stadium has played host to the Scottish FA Cup final on 13 occasions, five of which were replays:

1890	Queen's Park 2–1 Vale of Leven
1892	Celtic 5–1 Queen's Park *(replay)*
1893	Queen's Park 2–1 Celtic *(replay)*
1895	St Bernard's 2–1 Renton
1900	Celtic 4–3 Queen's Park
1901	Hearts 4–3 Celtic
1906	Hearts 1–0 Third Lanark
1910	Dundee 2–1 Clyde *(replay)*
1911	Celtic 2–0 Hamilton Academical *(replay)*
1912	Celtic 2–0 Clyde
1914	Celtic 4–1 Hibernian *(replay)*
1924	Airdrie 2–0 Hibernian
1997	Kilmarnock 1–0 Falkirk

✳ RANGERS SUNK BY THE WELL ✳

Motherwell won their first ever Scottish First Division championship in the 1931–32 season, beating Rangers by five clear points. "The Well" became the first club outside the Old Firm to win the title since Third Lanark's success 28 years earlier.

✳ A CHANGE OF RULES – 2 ✳

In the 1924–25 season – during which Rangers clinched their third consecutive Scottish First Division championship – the offside rule was changed. The rule change was straightforward and was to take effect from the 1926–27 season. Instead of three men being required to be between a player and the goal when he received a pass, only two players would now be required.

✳ UNLUCKY BREAK COSTS McCOIST RECORD ✳

Ally McCoist scored 34 league goals for Rangers in three different seasons – 1986–87, 1991–92 and 1992–93. During the 1992–93 season, McCoist was well on his way to smashing his record, until he broke his leg playing for Scotland against Portugal on 28 April 1993 in a World Cup qualifying game at Estadio da Luz, Lisbon. He missed the last five league games of the season, and the Scottish Cup final.

❈ UP FOR THE CUP (8) ❈

In the 1963–64 season, Rangers cleaned up domestically to win their first Treble in 15 years. The Scottish League Cup final saw a 5–0 drubbing of Morton, while Rangers won the league championship at a canter, by a mammoth 14 points from Kilmarnock. In the Scottish Cup, Rangers began their march to the final with a 5–0 away hammering of Stenhousemuir in the first round followed by a goal-fest at Ibrox in the second round and a 9–0 win over Duns. In the third round, Rangers beat Partick Thistle 3–0 at Ibrox and then beat Celtic 2–0 at Ibrox in the quarter-finals. After seeing off Dunfermline Athletic with a 1–0 win in the semi-final, Rangers wrapped up the Treble with a comfortable 3–1 win over Dundee in the final.

Scottish FA Cup Final
25 APRIL 1964, HAMPDEN PARK, GLASGOW
Rangers (0) 3   v.   Dundee (1) 1
(Millar (2), Brand)   (Cameron)

Att. 120,982

Rangers: Billy Ritchie, Bobby Shearer, Davie Provan, John Greig, Ronnie McKinnon, Jim Baxter, Willie Henderson, Tommy McLean, Jimmy Millar, Ralph Brand, Davie Wilson.

Did You Know That?
Rangers beat Celtic five times during the 1963–64 season: twice in the league, twice in the League Cup and also in the quarter-final of the Scottish Cup.

❈ RANGERS PLC ❈

In 1889, Rangers took the decision to become a company with their match secretary, William Wilton, becoming the club's first manager. The club also appointed its first board of directors, under the chairmanship of James Henderson.

❈ THE VIDEO GAME MASTER ❈

Along with football commentator John Motson, Ally McCoist added the commentry for the popular EA Sports FIFA Soccer video games series for many years. However, in 2006, EA Sports replaced McCoist and Motson with Andy Gray and Clive Tyldesley (for *FIFA 2006*).

❋ WIT AND WISDOM OF THE BLUES (12) ❋

"It was a fantasatic achievement, made even more special by the fact it was won at Parkhead."
Donald Findlay, *on Rangers completing the Treble at Celtic's ground*

❋ A REVIVED INTERNATIONAL CAREER ❋

When he was at Rangers, Davie Cooper won 20 international caps for Scotland. Despite his love for the club, Davie found himself with no option but to leave Ibrox to secure regular first-team football elsewhere. His former team-mate, Tommy McLean, persuaded him to sign for Motherwell. Davie played over 150 times for the "Steel Men" and was instrumental in helping Motherwell win their first major trophy in 39 years, the 1991 Scottish Cup final. Davie's move to Fir Park also revived his international career, and he went on to win a further four caps before an injury cost him his place and put an end to his international career.

❋ STRUTH TAKES CHARGE ❋

In May 1920, shortly after winning the Scottish First Division championship, the Rangers manager, William Wilton, lost his life in a boating accident and Bill Struth[†] took charge of the club. Struth would go on to guide the club to 18 league championships, ten Scottish Cups and two League Cups in his 34-year reign.

❋ THE ORANGE TWINS ❋

Frank and Ronald de Boer played alongside each other for no fewer than five teams:

Ajax *(Holland)* ❖ A-Rayyan *(Qatar)* ❖ Barcelona *(Spain)*
Glasgow Rangers ❖ Holland

❋ RANGERS AND CELTIC IN BED TOGETHER ❋

Graeme Souness and Kenny Dalglish were regular room-mates on Liverpool's away trips.

[†]*In the 1948–49 season, Bill Struth was also the first Rangers manager to win the domestic Treble – it was the first time the feat had been achieved in Scottish football history. Struth led Rangers to two further Doubles, in 1950 and 1953.*

❋ RANGERS XI OF THE 1960s ❋

1
Billy
RITCHIE

2
Bobby
SHEARER

3
Bill
PATERSON

4
Eric
CALDOW

5
Harry
DAVIS

6
Jim
BAXTER

7
Willie
HENDERSON

8
Ian
McMILLAN

9
James
FORREST

10
Ralph
BRAND

11
Davie
WILSON

Reserves
Eric *SORENSEN* • Kai *JOHANSEN* • Alex *SCOTT* • Dave *SMITH*
Alex *FERGUSON* • Orjan *PERSON*
Manager
Willie *WADDELL*

Did You Know That?
In the 1963 Scottish Cup final replay between Rangers and Celtic at
Hampden Park on 15 May 1963, Ralph Brand scored his second, and
Rangers' third goal, in a 3–0 win – Davie Wilson scored the other
Rangers goal – with 20 minutes of the game still to play. As soon as
Rangers' third hit the back of Frank Haffey's net, the King's Park End at
Hampden Park emptied as the Celtic fans headed home in disgust.

❋ THE MATCH ❋

In early 2004 and 2005, *The Match* appeared on Sky One television.
In the popular programme, the former England football team
manager, Graham Taylor, managed a football team called "The
Celebrities". Taylor's team had to play a match against a team of
football legends, who were managed by Sir Bobby Robson and who
included Ally McCoist and Matt Le Tissier. The show was hosted by
Mark Durden-Smith, Ulrika Jonsson (2004) and Zoe Ball (2005).
The Legends team won both games.

❋ 101 GOALS ❋

During the time Ally McCoist and Mark Hateley played in the same Rangers team together, they bagged 101 goals between them.

❋ A DOUBLE TREBLE ❋

Graeme Souness, who led Liverpool to three consecutive league championships during his captaincy of the Merseyside club (1982, 1983 and 1984), later led Rangers to three consecutive Scottish Premier League championships during his time as manager of the club (1989, 1990 and 1991).

❋ PENALTY SHOOT-OUT FIRST ❋

In 1988, the Scottish League Cup final was settled by a penalty shoot-out for the first time in the competition's history. Rangers drew 3–3 with Aberdeen at Hampden Park and won the penalty shoot-out 5–3 to win the Scottish League Cup for the 15th time.

❋ SCOTTISH LEAGUE CUP – OLD FIRM FINALS ❋

Rangers have met Celtic in the final of the Scottish League Cup[†] on 12 occasions. Rangers lead the way with eight wins to Celtic's four. All of the games have been played at Hampden Park, with three of them requiring extra time to settle them:

Year	Winners
2003	Rangers 2–1 Celtic
1991	Rangers 2–1 Celtic *(aet)*
1987	Rangers 2–1 Celtic
1984	Rangers 3–2 Celtic *(aet)*
1983	Celtic 2–1 Rangers
1978	Rangers 2–1 Celtic *(aet)*
1976	Rangers 1–0 Celtic
1971	Rangers 1–0 Celtic
1967	Celtic 1–0 Rangers
1966	Celtic 2–1 Rangers
1965	Rangers 2–1 Celtic
1958	Celtic 7–1 Rangers

[†] *Ibrox Park has hosted the Scottish League Cup final on two occasions: 1998 Celtic 3–0 Dundee United; 1995 Raith Rovers 2–2 Celtic (Raith won 6–5 on penalties)*

❄ RANGERS IN EUROPE (2) ❄

In 1967, Rangers reached their second European Cup-Winners' Cup final. Their European campaign got off to a good start with a 5–1 aggregate win over Glentoran in the first round. That was followed by a 2–1 aggregate win over Borussia Dortmund in the second round before they narrowly squeezed past Real Zaragoza in the quarter-finals – they advanced to the semi-finals after a lucky coin toss fell in their favour. Rangers beat Slavia Sofia 1–0 both at home and away to book a final place against Bayern Munich. However, Rangers lost 0–1, after extra-time, to the Germans at the Nurnbergerstadion in Nuremberg.

EUROPEAN CUP-WINNERS' CUP FINAL 1967
31 MAY 1967, NURNBERGERSTADION, NUREMBERG
Bayern Munich (0) 1   v.   Rangers (0) 0 *(aet)*
(Roth)
Att. 69,000
Bayern Munich: Maier, Nowak, Kupferschmidt, Beckenbauer, Olk, Roth, Koulmann, Nafziger, Ohlhauser, Muller, Brenninger.
Rangers: Norrie Martin, Kai Johansen, Sandy Jardine, Peter McKinnon, Davie Provan, Alex Smith, John Greig, Willie Henderson, John Hynd, David Smith, Willie Johnston.

Did You Know That?
In 1933, the National Socialists began to use the Nurnbergerstadion as a practice marching arena for the Hitler Youth.

❄ I PLAYED FOR BOTH ❄

The following players played for both Old Firm sides:

Tom Sinclair................Rangers 1904–06 and Celtic 1906–07
Robert Campbell................Celtic 1905–06 and Rangers 1906–14
Willie Kivlichan................Rangers 1905–07 and Celtic 1907–11
Hugh Shaw................Rangers 1905–06 and Celtic 1906–07
David Taylor................Rangers 1906–11 and Celtic 1918–19
    (as a guest player)
Davie McLean................Celtic 1907–09 and Rangers 1918–19
James Young................Celtic 1917–18 and Rangers 1917–18
Alfie Conn Jr................Rangers 1968–74 and Celtic 1977–79
Scott Duncan................Rangers 1913–18 and Celtic 1918–19
    (as a guest player)
Maurice Johnston................Celtic 1984–87 and Rangers 1989–92

❋ AFTER RANGERS ❋

The following Rangers players/managers all had another career after football:

Ally Scott	Insurance agent
Kai Johansen	Pub landlord/Players' agent
Ally McCoist	Television commentator
Willie Waddell	Journalist

❋ FRENCH TRIBUTE TO COOPER ❋

At the beginning of the 1988–89 season, a testimonial match was held for Davie Cooper at Ibrox Stadium. Rangers entertained the French side Girondins de Bordeaux in a game they won 3–2 in front of 43,000 adoring Cooper fans.

❋ LEGEND WAS ALMOST A JAM TART ❋

When John Greig was growing up, he supported his hometown club, Heart of Midlothian, and had his heart set on joining them. However, when Rangers came knocking on his parents' door, his father persuaded the young Greig to sign for them.

❋ RAE TO THE RESCUE ❋

In 2005, Alex Rae lent a helping hand to Capability Scotland's new campaign, providing the slogan being "Can't is a four letter word". Scotland's leading disability organization released a number of T-shirts and wristbands bearing the slogan to help raise money to support its work of providing a range of flexible services which support disabled people of all ages in their everyday lives.

❋ THE BLUES BROTHERS ❋

In the late 1890s and early 1900s, a number of Glasgow Rangers players signed for Everton. The Blues Brothers link continued during the 1990s, when Everton obtained Ian Durrant and Duncan Ferguson from Rangers in 1994, while the Everton captain Dave Watson's testimonial match was against Rangers in the 1997–98 season. The former Rangers manager Walter Smith later brought former Ibrox stars Paul Gascoigne and Richard Gough to Goodison Park during his time at the helm of the club.

❋ NINE-IN-A-ROW PLAYERS ❋

The following 86 players all played for Rangers during their nine championships in a row:

Jorg Albertz	David Hagen	Gordan Petric
Joachim Bjorklund	Mark Hateley	Steven Pressley
Erik Bo Anderson	Pieter Huistra	Brian Reid
Basile Boli	Terry Hurlock	Paul Rideout
Gary Bollan	Mo Johnston	David Robertson
Steven Boyack	David Kirkwood	Lee Robertson
John Brown	Oleg Kuznetsov	Sandy Robertson
Terry Butcher	Brian Laudrup	Sebastian Rozental
Neil Caldwell	Kevin MacDonald	Oleg Salenko
Alec Cleland	Ally Maxwell	Colin Scott
Davie Cooper	Ian McCall	Greg Shields
Neale Cooper	Stuart McCall	Theo Snelders
Tom Cowan	Ally McCoist	Graeme Souness
Andy Dibble	Brian McGinty	Nigel Spackman
Davie Dodds	John McGregor	John Spencer
Kevin Drinkell	Derek McInnes	Mel Sterland
Gordon Durie	Paul McKnight	Trevor Steven
Iain Durrant	Alan McLaren	Gary Stevens
Barry Ferguson	Dave McPherson	Billy Thomson
Derek Ferguson	Gary McSwegan	Peter Van Vossen
Duncan Ferguson	Alexei Mikhailitchenko	Chris Vinnicombe
Ian Ferguson	Charlie Miller	Nicky Walker
Darren Fitzgerald	Craig Moore	Mark Walters
Paul Gascoigne	John Morrow	Stephen Watson
Bonni Ginzburg	Stuart Munro	Ray Wilkins
Andy Goram	Neil Murray	Scott Wilson
Dale Gordon	Jimmy Nicholl	Fraser Wishart
Richard Gough	Scott Nisbet	Chris Woods
Andy Gray		Stephen Wright

❋ RANGERS £4 MILLION ARAB TERROR ❋

When Duncan Ferguson moved from Dundee United[†] to Rangers, "The Terrors" or "The Arabs" received a club record fee – £4 million.

[†]*In 1909, following the demise of Dundee Harp, the Irish Community in Dundee formed a new football club, calling it Dundee Hibernian, and took over Clepington Park (later renamed Tannadice Park) from Dundee Wanderers. In 1923, the club changed its name to Dundee United.*

❉ GOLDEN BOOTS ❉

Although the Golden Boot Award[†] was not presented before 1968, the following Rangers players would have won the award had it been in existence at the time:

Season	Name	Goals
1898–99	Robert Hamilton	25
1903–04	Robert Hamilton	28
1933–34	Jimmy Smith	41
1964–65	Jim Forrest	30

❉ 'GERS STAR SCORES WINNER FOR BRAZIL ❉

On 30 June 1973, Scotland took on the world champions Brazil in a friendly at Hampden Park. Derek Johnstone scored the only goal of the game, an own goal, to hand Brazil a 1–0 win.

❉ CELTIC SEEDED THANKS TO RANGERS ❉

Celtic were awarded the final seeding, 16th place, for the final qualifying round in the 2002–03 Champions League as a direct result of Rangers' long run in the previous season's UEFA Cup.

❉ IN THE BEGINNING ❉

In 1872, Peter Campbell, William McBeath, Moses McNeil and Tom Vallance stood and watched a group of men play a game of football on Glasgow Green's Flesher's Haugh. The four friends decided there and then to form their own football team and, as a result, Glasgow Rangers Football Club was formed. In the beginning, three of McNeil's six brothers (Harry, Peter and William) joined Moses in the early Rangers side.

❉ CHARLES HEGGIE ❉

Rangers' Charles Heggie holds the club record for goals scored for Scotland in relation to the number of games played. Charles scored four times for Scotland in a 7–2 win over Ireland on 20 March 1886. Remarkably, it was his only cap.

[†] *Between 1991 and 1996, no Golden Boot was awarded, so Ally McCoist missed out on receiving the award in 1991–92 (34 goals) and 1992–93 (34 goals) when he was Europe's top goalscorer.*

✳ WIT AND WISDOM OF THE BLUES (13) ✳

"Nothing prepared me for what it was like. It was the greatest footballing experience of my life."
Jorg Albertz, on his first Old Firm game

✳ GAZZA THE PRANKSTER (4) ✳

1. When he was an apprentice at Newcastle United, he once took Kevin Keegan's football boots home to show off to his mates and left them on the Newcastle Underground by mistake.
2. During a stay at a Scottish hotel, he drove his four-wheel-drive Jeep across its golf course, much to the annoyance of the golfers.
3. He once pretended he could speak Danish when he was introduced to the president of Denmark's Football Association. When he was then invited to say something in Danish, he imitated the Swedish chef from *The Muppet Show*.
4. After Italia '90, a tournament in which Sheffield Wednesday's Chris Waddle had starred, he walked into a Sheffield barbershop and demanded a "Waddle cut".
5. When he was at Middlesbrough, he walked into the canteen and ordered lunch wearing nothing but his football socks.

✳ RANGERS' FIRST GAME ✳

Glasgow Rangers' first ever game was in May 1872 and was played against Callender FC on Flesher's Haugh, Glasgow. It ended in a scoreless draw. However, Rangers called themselves "Argyle" for the game and it wasn't until their second game that they adopted the Rangers name.

✳ THE BIRTH OF THE CLUB'S NAME ✳

After playing their first game as "Argyle", Moses McNeil suggested a name change to "Rangers", having seen the name in a book about English rugby. Everyone agreed and in their second game, now wearing a light blue kit and bearing the name of Rangers, they beat Clyde 11–0.

✳ THE FIRST EVER OLD FIRM LEAGUE GAME ✳

The first ever league meeting between the Old Firm took place on 21 March 1891 at Celtic Park and ended in a 2–2 draw.

❋ RANGERS IN EUROPE (3) ❋

In the 1972 European Cup-Winners' Cup final, Rangers were up against the mighty Russian side, Dynamo Moscow, in Barcelona's magnificent Nou Camp stadium. This was Rangers' third ECWC final and although the stadium could accommodate 110,000 fans, only a crowd of 40,000 turned up – 25,000 of that number were Rangers fans. When Rangers took the lead midway through the first half, a number of Rangers fans spilled on to the pitch and play was held up for a while. Two goals in the second half from Willie Johnston finally saw Rangers emerge from Celtic's European shadow.

European Cup-Winners' Cup Final 1972

24 MAY 1972, ESTADIO CAMP NOU, BARCELONA

Rangers (2) 3 v. Dynamo Moscow (0) 2

(Stein, W. Johnston 2) (Estrekov, Makovikov)

Att. 35,000

Rangers: Peter McCloy, Sandy Jardine, John Greig, Derek Johnstone, Willie Mathieson, David Smith, Alfie Conn, Alex MacDonald, Tommy McLean, Colin Stein, Willie Johnston.

Moscow Dynamo: Pilgui, Basalayev, Dolmatov, Zykov, Dolbonosov (Gershkovich), Zhukov, Baydachny, Yakubik (Eshtrekov), Sabo, Makhovikov, Yevryuzhikhin

Did You Know That?

It had taken Rangers 16 years and 83 European matches to win their first European trophy. After the final, UEFA banned Rangers from European competition for two years, later reduced to a year on appeal, after Rangers fans had run on to the pitch one minute before full time, causing the referee to end the game early.

❋ CELEBRITY 'GERS ❋

Jonathan Watson........*comedian and impressionist*
Colin Montgomerie........*golfer*
Patsy Kensit........*actress*
Gordon Ramsay........*chef*
Andy "The Viking" Fordham........*darts champion*
Midge Ure........*Band Aid organizer*
Nick Nairn........*chef*
Carol Smillie........*TV presenter*
Alan McGee........*founded Creation records and discovered Oasis*

❋ HAT-TRICK SCORERS FOR SCOTLAND ❋

Only six Rangers players have ever scored a hat-trick for Scotland and Bob Hamilton is the only 'Ger to have scored two hat-tricks for Scotland.

Player	*Opponent*	*Date*
Colin Stein	Cyprus	17 May 1969
Alex Scott	Northern Ireland	7 October 1961
Alec Smith	Wales	15 March 1902
Bob Hamilton	Ireland	1 March 1902
Bob Hamilton	Ireland	23 February 1901 *(4 goals)*
John Barker	Wales	18 March 1893
Charles Heggie	Ireland	20 March 1886

❋ JAGS GIVE 'GERS THE BLUES ❋

In the 1953–54 season, Rangers finished below Partick Thistle in the Scottish League for the first and only time in the club's history. "The Jags" finished the campaign in third place†, one position ahead of Rangers.

❋ GREEN AND BLUE MOJO ❋

The following England internationals have all played for an Old Firm team during their career and appear, as close as possible, in the position they played for their club and country:

1.	Chris Woods	Rangers
2.	Gary Stevens	Rangers
3.	Michael Ball	Rangers
4.	Ray Wilkins	Rangers
5.	Terry Butcher	Rangers
6.	Chris Sutton	Celtic
7.	Trevor Steven	Rangers
8.	Paul Gascoigne	Rangers
9.	Mark Hateley	Rangers
10.	Alan Thompson	Celtic
11.	Steve Guppy	Celtic

†Had Rangers lost away to Hibernian on the last day of the season, they would have finished the season in eighth place, their lowest ever league placing. However, the 2–2 draw at Easter Road meant that Rangers finished fourth, although only on goal difference, as four other teams shared the same points total (34): Hibernian, East Fife, Dundee and Clyde.

❋ IF YOU KNOW YOUR HISTORY ❋

Glasgow Rangers were founded when four men – Peter Campbell, William McBeath, Moses McNeil and Peter McNeil – got together with the intention of forming their own football club. The Rangers name was taken from an English rugby club. Rangers FC were formed in 1873, when the club held its first formal meeting to elect club officials. In 1877, Rangers reached their first Scottish Cup final, losing to Vale of Leven. In 1890, the Scottish League began its inaugural season and, at this time, Rangers played their home games at Ibrox Park, having previously played them at Burnbank and Kinning Park. On 16 August 1890, Rangers played their first ever league game, with Hearts providing the opposition. At the end of the inaugural Scottish First Division season, 1980–91, Rangers finished level on points with Dumbarton and the championship was shared. In 1894, Rangers won the Scottish Cup for the first time, beating Celtic 3–1 at Hampden Park. In 1898–99, Rangers won the first of their world record 51 championships outright by winning all 18 of their league games. In 1899, Rangers moved permanently to Ibrox Park. In the 1956–57 season, Rangers played in Europe for the first time when they entered the European Cup. In 1961, Rangers became the first Scottish club to reach a European final, losing on aggregate to Fiorentina in the inaugural European Cup-Winners' Cup final. On 2 January 1971, the blackest day in Rangers' history occurred when, following an Old Firm game, 66 people died and 145 were injured in a terrifying crush at Ibrox Park[†]. In 1972, Rangers won the European Cup-Winners' Cup, beating Dynamo Moscow in the final. The club's greatest ever achievement is undoubtedly the nine Scottish championships they won in a row between 1988–89 and 1996–97 under Graeme Souness and Walter Smith.

❋ A GIANT OF A PLAYER ❋

George "Corky" Young was Rangers' tallest captain until Terry Butcher was given the role. He stood 6ft 2in and weighed 15 stones. A giant of man, he was a rock in defence, winning six league championships, four Scottish Cups, two Scottish League Cups and, at the time, a record 53 caps for Scotland, captaining his country 48 times. Aged just 15, he signed as an amateur for Rangers in 1937, turned professional in 1941 and remained at the club until he retired in 1957.

[†]*In the same year that the Ibrox Disaster occurred, 20 people lost their lives in the Clarkston gas explosion.*

❈ THE TENNENTS' SIXES ❈

The Tennents' Sixes was an annual indoor football tournament, held from 1984 to 1993, that was contested in January each year by Scotland's senior clubs. The tournament was sponsored by Tennent Caledonian Breweries and was organized by the SFA. The inaugural tournament took place at Coasters Arena in Falkirk in 1984 with Rangers claiming the cup. In 1985, the tournament moved to the Ingliston Showground near Edinburgh, and the remaining eight tournaments were all held at the Scottish Exhibition and Conference Centre in Glasgow. Along with Rangers, Aberdeen and Hearts won the tournament twice, while Motherwell were beaten finalists on four occasions. After Partick Thistle's success in 1993, Tennent Caledonian Breweries withdrew their sponsorship, thus bringing down the curtain on the event. The winners were:

1984	Rangers
1985	Hearts
1986	Aberdeen
1987	Aberdeen
1988	Dundee
1989	Rangers
1990	Hibernian
1991	Hearts
1992	Celtic
1993	Partick Thistle

❈ RANGERS' 100TH IS ALLY'S 200TH ❈

On 2 May 1992, Rangers beat Aberdeen 2–0 at Pittodrie in the final league game of the season. Ally McCoist's[†] first goal in the game was Rangers' 100th league goal of the season and was also his 200th goal for the club.

❈ WORST EVER RUN WITHOUT A WIN ❈

When Hibernian beat Rangers 2–1 at Easter Road in the SPL on 27 November 2005, it was Rangers' eighth consecutive game without a victory, the worst non-win sequence in Rangers' 133-year history. It reached ten before the 'Gers beat Kilmarnock – and they went on a run of seven wins and a draw in eight games.

[†]*In the 1991–92 season, Ally scored 41 goals in all competitions, won both the Sports Writers' Player of the Year Award and the Managers' Player of the Year Award and Europe's Golden Boot.*

✹ UP FOR THE CUP (9) ✹

One week after Rangers had lost the 1972–73 Scottish First Division championship to Celtic by a single point, the Old Firm were at Hampden Park for the Scottish Cup final. Rangers' Scottish Cup run began with a 1–0 win over Dundee United in the third round at Ibrox followed by a 2–1 away win over Hibs in a fourth-round replay. In the quarter-finals, they beat Airdrieonians 2–0 at Ibrox and then saw off Ayr United with a 2–0 win at Hampden Park in the semi-finals. In the final, goals from Alfie Conn, Derek Parlane and Tom Forsyth handed them a 3–2 win over their archrivals to hand the Ibrox men some consolation for their disappointment in the league.

SCOTTISH FA CUP FINAL
5 MAY 1973, HAMPDEN PARK, GLASGOW
Rangers (1) 3   v.   Celtic (1) 2
(Conn, Parlane, Forsyth)   (Dalglish, Connelly (pen))
Att. 122,714

Rangers: Peter McCloy, Sandy Jardine, John Greig,
Derek Johnstone, Willie Mathieson, Tom Forsyth, Alfie Conn,
Alex MacDonald, Tommy McLean, Derek Parlane, Quinton Young.

Did You Know That?
It was Rangers' first Scottish Cup success in seven years and the 20th time they had won the trophy in their history. Rangers have a total of 31 Scottish Cup wins.

✹ RANGERS MAKE EUROPEAN HISTORY ✹

Alex McLeish put his domestic worries in the Scottish Premier League to one side as he guided Rangers into the second phase of the Champions League following a 1–1 home draw with Inter Milan on 6 December 2005[†]. The Brazilian sensation Adriano put Inter Milan in front when he headed home from five yards, but then Thomas Buffel sent Peter Lovenkrands clear to race in on goal and fire home the equalizer past Francesco Toldo. With only five minutes of the game remaining, Cristiano Zanetti of Inter Milan was sent off. Rangers' qualification from their group, headed by the Italians, entered their name in the history books as they were the first Scottish side to progress beyond the group stages of the competition.

'Prior to qualifying for the second phase of the Champions League, Rangers had not won a game in ten matches – the worst non-winning run in the club's history.

❈ RICHARD GOUGH ❈

Richard Gough was born in Stockholm, Sweden, on 5 April 1962, but grew up in South Africa and began his career at the Wits University club. Aged only 18, he travelled to Glasgow for a trial with Rangers, but failed to impress and was allowed to leave by John Greig's coaching staff. He went on loan to Charlton Athletic for a while, a team his father had played for, returned to South Africa and then, in 1980, was signed by Dundee United. He was a class act for Dundee United in the heart of their defence for the next six seasons and helped them clinch the Scottish League championship in 1982–83. He was excellent in the air, instinctively knew when to release the ball from defence and was quick on his feet.

In 1986, after 165 games and 23 goals for the Tannadice club, Gough joined Tottenham Hotspur for £750,000. His time in the English First Division was not an enjoyable experience and, midway through the 1987–88 season, he returned to Scotland when Graeme Souness made him the club's first £1 million-plus player (£1.1 million). On 10 October 1987, he made his league debut for Rangers at right-back, ironically against Dundee United in a 0–1 defeat, and then, in his second game for the club, he scored in the 2–2 draw with Celtic.

Gough played in all the famous nine-in-a-row championships, making 263 league appearances, 77 more than any other Rangers player during the same period. Although two other players played in all nine of Rangers' successful championship campaigns (1988–89 to 1996–97), namely Ian Ferguson and Ally McCoist, it was Gough alone who collected nine championship-winners' medals. In 1990, he took over the captaincy of the club from his defensive partner, Terry Butcher, and so led the team to seven consecutive titles, in addition to winning three Scottish Cups and six Scottish League Cups – an impressive medal haul by any player's standards. During his career, Gough won 61 caps for Scotland – 28 of them during his Ibrox days – and played a total of 427 games for Rangers.

In 1997, despite the desire and appetite to aim for ten championships in a row, Gough, then aged 35, knew that it was time to leave: it is a testimony to the man's greatness. He joined the Kansas City Wizards followed by the San Jose Clash in the USA's Major League Soccer. At the end of the 1997 MLS season, he returned to Ibrox for one more season. Later in his career, he played for Everton and Nottingham Forest and, on 30 November 2004, he landed his first managerial job with Livingston in the SPL. However, despite saving the club from relegation, he resigned in May 2005.

WIT AND WISDOM OF THE BLUES (14)

"You have to remember that we have our blue noses to go along with our orange shirts."
***Dick Advocaat**, after many Rangers fans had worn Dutch tops at the 2000 Scottish Cup final*

NICKNAMES

Nickname	*Player*
Wee Willie	Willie Henderson
Slim Jim	Jim Baxter
The Wee Blue Devil	Alan Morton
Rhino	Don Kitchebrand
The Iron Curtain	Rangers' defence back in the 1930s
The Wee Prime Minister	Ian McMillan
The Hammer	Jorg Albertz
Corky	George Young
Barry	Alex McLeish
The Goalie	Andy Goram
Julie	Ian Andrews
Bud	Willie Johnston
Tiger	Jock Shaw
Dudley/The Judge	Ally McCoist
Attila	Mark Hateley
Jaws	Tom Forsyth
Lighthouse	Peter McCloy

FIRST EVER FLOODLIT GAME

The first ever Scottish League game under floodlit conditions was played at Ochilview Park, Stenhousemuir, on 3 January 1953, when Rangers beat Third Lanark 2–0. It would be a further year before Rangers installed floodlights at Ibrox.

LEAGUE CUP RECORD-HOLDER

When Rangers beat Hearts 4–3 in the 1996 Scottish League Cup, Ally McCoist collected his ninth winners' medal in the competition – a record – in his tenth final appearance, which bettered Billy McNeill's tally of nine finals. Ally's two goals in the game meant that he had scored a total of eight goals in Scottish League Cup finals, which is also a record.

✳ RANGERS XI OF THE 1970s ✳

1
Peter
McCLOY

2
Sandy
JARDINE

3
Willie
MATHIESON

4
John
GREIG

5
Derek
JOHNSTONE

6
Ronnie
McKINNON

7
Tommy
McLEAN

8
Alfie
CONN

9
Colin
STEIN

10
Alex
MacDONALD

11
Willie
JOHNSTON

Reserves
Stewart *KENNEDY* • Colin *JACKSON* • Alex *MILLER*
Quinton *YOUNG* • Derek *PARLANE*
Manager
John *GREIG*

Did You Know That?
When Rangers beat Celtic 3–2 on 5 May 1973 in the Scottish Cup final, it was the first time that a member of the Royal Family had attended a Scottish Cup final. Princess Alexandra attended.

✳ A BLUE 2003–04 OLD FIRM ✳

The 2003–04 season was the first time in the history of the Scottish Premier League, dating back to the 1975–76 season, that Rangers had lost all four league games to Celtic.

✳ RANGERS' FOREIGN LEGION ✳

On 1 October 2003, Rangers drew 1–1 away to Panathinaikos of Greece in the second game of their Champions League group E campaign. The Rangers team on the night did not contain a single Scot, including the substitutes. It was the first time in the history of the club that a Rangers team was composed entirely of non-Scottish-born players.

❋ EUROPEAN CONSISTENCY ❋

Rangers are one of only 15 clubs to have played in one of the three major European competitions (excluding the Intertoto Cup) for at least 20 consecutive seasons[†]:

48	Barcelona	(1957–58 to 2005–06)
42	Anderlecht	(1964–65 to 2005–06)
41	Benfica	(1960–61 to 2000–01)
32	FC Porto	(1974–75 to 2005–06)
	PSV Eindhoven	(1974–75 to 2005–06)
29	Sporting Lisbon	(1977–78 to 2005–06)
28	Juventus	(1963–64 to 1990–91)
25	Rangers	(1981–82 to 2005–06)
24	Ajax	(1966–67 to 1989–90)
	Crvena Zvezda (Red Star) Belgrade	(1968–69 to 1991–92)
	Spartak Moscow	(1980–81 to 2003–04)
23	Sparta Prague	(1983–84 to 2005–06)
22	Real Madrid	(1955–56 to 1976–77)
21	Liverpool	(1964–65 to 1984–85)
20	Austria Vienna	(1976–77 to 1995–96)

❋ NIVEN THE HERO ❋

In the 1953 Scottish Cup final, George Niven, Rangers' young goalkeeper, dived at the feet of Aberdeen's Paddy Buckley and injured himself. He was carried off and George Young, the Rangers captain, went into goal in his place. Eighteen minutes later, Niven reappeared wearing a protective leather helmet and helped Rangers to a 1–0 win.

❋ CHEAP CENTENARY CELEBRATIONS ❋

At the start of the 1973–74 season, Rangers played Arsenal at Ibrox to celebrate Rangers' centenary. As a gesture to the fans, the club reduced the admission price for the game – ranging from 5p to 20p – which resulted in a bumper attendance of 71,000. Arsenal spoilt the celebrations, however, winning 2–1 with two very late goals.

[†]*Liverpool were banned, along with all English teams, from European competition from 1985–86 to 1990–91 as a result of the Heysel Stadium disaster in 1985; in 1989, Ajax were also banned from European competition for two years as a result of crowd trouble; Crvena Zvezda Belgrade were banned from European competition in 1992–93 as a result of a United Nations boycott.*

✳ WE ARE THE CHAMPIONS (9) ✳

Rangers started the 1974–75 league season in fine form and beat Celtic 2–1 at Celtic Park in only the third game of the campaign. The Old Firm win gave the players tremendous confidence and it took 13 games before anyone could beat them – with Hibernian ending the sequence with a 1–0 win at Ibrox. By the turn of the year, Rangers trailed Celtic by two points, but a magnificent 3–1 Old Firm win at Ibrox gave them the momentum they sought and they remained unbeaten in the league until the title had been secured. They finished seven points ahead of Hibernian and 11 ahead of Celtic.

Scottish League Division One
1974–75

		P	W	D	L	F	A	W	D	L	F	A	Pts
1.	**Rangers**	34	14	1	2	39	15	11	5	1	47	18	56
2.	Hibernian	34	12	2	3	41	16	8	7	2	28	21	49
3.	Celtic	34	11	2	4	47	20	9	3	5	34	21	45
4.	Dundee United	34	10	5	2	41	19	9	2	6	31	24	45
5.	Aberdeen	34	9	6	2	42	20	7	3	7	24	23	41
6.	Dundee	34	11	1	5	32	17	5	5	7	16	25	38
7.	Ayr United	34	9	5	3	29	27	5	3	9	21	34	36
8.	Heart of Midlothian	34	8	6	3	24	16	3	7	7	23	36	35
9.	St Johnstone	34	8	4	5	27	20	3	8	6	14	24	34
10.	Motherwell	34	8	2	7	30	23	6	3	8	22	34	33
11.	Airdrieonians	34	7	7	3	26	20	4	2	11	17	35	31
12.	Kilmarnock	34	5	7	5	26	29	3	8	6	26	39	31
13.	Partick Thistle	34	7	5	5	27	31	3	5	9	21	31	30
14.	Dumbarton	34	3	5	9	19	24	4	5	8	25	31	24
15.	Dunfermline Athletic	34	3	6	8	24	32	4	3	10	22	34	23
16.	Clyde	34	4	6	7	25	30	2	4	11	15	33	22
17.	Morton	34	4	5	8	17	28	2	5	10	14	34	22
18.	Arbroath	34	4	5	8	20	27	1	2	14	14	39	17

✳ COOPER ALMOST A SEAGULL ✳

In the summer of 1980, Alan Mullery, the manager of Brighton and Hove Albion, nicknamed "The Seagulls", made a bid for both Davie Cooper and Gordon Smith. John Greig, the Rangers manager at the time, was only prepared to allow one of the players to leave Ibrox and Mullery chose Smith.

❋ THE FAMOUS GLASGOW RANGERS ❋

As I was walking doon the Copland Road,
I met a bunch o' strangers,
They said to me, you going to see,
The famous Glasgow Rangers.
So I took them up to Ibrox Park,
To see the flags unfurl,
After that display they had to say
They're the champions of the world.

Some people they sing songs about
The land that they adore
And some of how they fought and won
Their countries' greatest wars,
Some others still seem quite content
To use another theme,
But I can sing a song about
A famous football team.

As I was walking doon the Copland Road,
I met a bunch o' strangers,
They said to me, you going to see,
The famous Glasgow Rangers.

❋ WIT AND WISDOM OF THE BLUES (15) ❋

"In training it was the English versus the Scots. Coisty came in our
team because, as I told him at the time, he had played two games for
the Sunderland reserves."
Terry Butcher

❋ A STICKY DEBUT ❋

Although Lorenzo Amoruso made his competitive debut for Rangers
in an Old Firm derby, his first game for Rangers was at Goodison
Park[†] against Everton, nicknamed "The Toffees", in David Watson's
testimonial match on 16 July 1997. Amoruso later played for Blackburn
Rovers against Everton at Goodison Park.

---

*[†] Everton played at Anfield before Liverpool FC was even formed. In 1892, Everton fell out with
the owner of Anfield, John Houlding, over a rent increase. Everton moved to Goodison Park and
Houlding went on to found his own team, Liverpool Football Club.*

⚽ RANGERS IN EUROPE: 1998–99 TO 2005–06 ❋

Season	Comp.	Round	Opponents	Home	Away	Agg.
1998–99	UEFA	pre 1	Shelbourne	2–0	5–3	7–3
		pre 2	PAOK Salonika	2–0	0–0	2–0
		1st	Beitar Jerusalem	4–2	1–1	5–3
		2nd	Bayer Leverkusen	1–1	2–1	3–2
		3rd	Parma	1–1	1–3	2–4
1999–00	EC	pre 1	FC Haka	3–0	4–1	7–1
		pre 2	Parma	2–0	0–1	2–1
		GS	Valencia	1–2	2–0	
		GS	PSV Eindhoven	4–1	1–0	
		GS	Bayern Munich	1–1	0–1	

(Failed to qualify for next stage of Champions League. Entered into UEFA Cup)

	UEFA	3rd	Borussia Dortmund	2–0	0–2	2–2

(Borussia Dortmund won 3–1 on penalties)

2000–01	EC	pre 1	FKB Kaunas	4–1	0–0	4–1
		pre 2	Herfloge	3–0	3–0	6–0
		GS	Sturm Graz	5–0	0–2	
		GS	Monaco	2–2	1–0	
		GS	Galatasaray	0–0	2–3	

(Failed to qualify for next stage of Champions League. Entered into UEFA Cup)

	UEFA	3rd	FC Kaiserslautern	1–0	0–3	1–3
2001–02	EC	pre 1	NK Maribor	3–1	3–0	6–1
		pre 2	Fenerbahce	0–0	1–2	1–2

(Failed to qualify for group stages of Champions League. Entered into UEFA Cup)

	UEFA	1st	Anzhi Makhachkala			1–0

(one-off game in Poland)

		2nd	Moscow Dynamo	3–1	4–1	7–1
		3rd	Paris S.G.	0–0	0–0	0–0

(Rangers won 4–3 on penalties)

		4th	Feyenoord	1–1	2–3	3–4
2002–03	UEFA	1st	Viktoria Zizkov	3–1	0–2	3–3

(Viktoria Zizkov won on the away-goals rule)

2003–04	EC	pre 3	FC Copenhagen	1–1	2–1	3–2
		GS	VfB Stuttgart	2–1	0–1	
		GS	Panathinakos	1–3	1–1	
		GS	Manchester United	0–1	0–3	
2004–05	EC	pre 3	CSKA Moscow	1–1	1–2	2–3
2005–06	EC	pre 3	Anorthosis	2–1	2–1	4–2

Season	Comp.	Round	Opponents	Home	Away	Agg.
	EC	GS	Porto	3–2	1–1	
			Inter Milan	1–1	0–1	
			Artmedia	0–0	2–2	
		2nd	Villarreal	2–2	1–1	3–3

(Villarreal won on the away-goals rule)

Key: *EC – European Cup/Champions League (GS = Group Stage); UEFA – UEFA Cup*

❉ CUP DUMPING ❉

Hibernian beat Rangers 3–0 at Ibrox on 4 February 2006 to dump them out of the Scottish Cup.

❉ RANGERS BEAT ENGLISH CUP WINNERS ❉

At the end of the 1893–94 season, Rangers, the Scottish Cup holders, played several friendly matches. They travelled south of the border to beat Leicester Fosse 2–1 and then recorded a 3–1 home win over Notts County, the winners of the 1894 English FA Cup after they beat Bolton Wanderers 4–1 in the final.

❉ THE DISCIPLINARIAN ❉

After Bill Struth[†] had been appointed Rangers' second manager in 1920, he guided them to 18 league championship titles, which included the amazing statistic of winning 14 titles in 19 years before the Second World War. In 1928, Struth managed Rangers to their first league and cup Double and, in 1949, he guided them to their first ever Treble. Struth was a renowned disciplinarian, insisting that his players wore a shirt and tie when they arrived for training. In 1947, he was made a director at Rangers and, in 1954, after stepping down as manager, he was appointed vice-chairman.

❉ BLUE REPLACES A GREEN AT REDS ❉

After guiding Rangers to four Scottish Premier League titles (1987, 1989, 1990 and 1991) and four Scottish League Cups, Graeme Souness left Ibrox to return to Liverpool as manager in April 1991.

[†] It is said that Bill Struth used to watch the players arrive at Ibrox on a matchday from the windows of the Main Stand. If he ever spotted a player walking into Ibrox with his hands in his pockets, he would turn that player away and make him walk back down the street and approach Ibrox a second time, this time with his hands firmly placed by his side.

❊ UP FOR THE CUP (10) ❊

Although finishing in a disappointing third place in the Scottish Premier League and having suffered an early Scottish League Cup exit to Aberdeen, the Rangers fans had cause to celebrate at the end of the season when Rangers won the Scottish Cup final after a replay. On their way to Hampden glory, Rangers beat Airdrieonians 5–0 away in the third round and St Johnstone 3–1 in a fourth-round replay, after a 3–3 away draw. In the quarter-finals, Hibs were swept aside 3–1 at Ibrox and that was followed by a 2–1 semi-final win over Morton at Celtic Park. The final against Dundee United at Hampden Park ended in a 0–0 draw before Rangers ran out 4–1 winners in the replay.

SCOTTISH FA CUP FINAL (REPLAY)
12 MAY 1981, HAMPDEN PARK, GLASGOW

Rangers (3) 4　　v.　　Dundee United (1) 1
(Cooper, Russell,　　　　　(Dodds)
McDonald (2))

Att. 43,099

Rangers: Jim Stewart, Sandy Jardine, Ally Dawson, Tom Forsyth, Gregor Stevens, Jim Bett, Davie Cooper, Bobby Russell, Derek Johnstone, Ian Redford, John McDonald.

Did You Know That?
St Johnstone's goal in their 3–1 fourth-round replay defeat at Ibrox was scored by a certain Ally McCoist.
have

❊ NINE-IN-A-ROW DOUBLE ❊

Rangers may have won nine Scottish League championships in a row between 1988–89 and 1996–97, but they achieved a similar feat from 1938–39 to 1946–47. However, six were unofficial wartime titles.

❊ BLUES TURN HAMPDEN ORANGE ❊

On 27 May 2000, Rangers beat Aberdeen 4–0 at Hampden Park in the Scottish Cup final. Thousands of Rangers fans turned up to the game wearing Holland strips in tribute to the team's Dutch contingent, one of whom, Arthur Numan, was captain for the day in his last game for the club. The game has since been dubbed "The Oranje Final".

❀ SCOTTISH PREMIER DIVISION CHAMPIONS ❀

The 1975–76 season saw the beginning of the new Scottish Premier Division[†] that lasted until the end of the 1997–98 season. Rangers won 12 of the 23 championships in the following years: 1976, 1978, 1987, 1989, 1990, 1991, 1992, 1993, 1994, 1995, 1996 and 1997.

❀ RANGERS LEVEL WITH LINFIELD ❀

Rangers share the record for having won the highest number of domestic Doubles with Linfield of Northern Ireland. Here is the all-time leader table:

Club	Nation	Number of Doubles
Linfield	Northern Ireland	17
Rangers	Scotland	17
Celtic	Scotland	13
HB	Faroe Islands	12
Muharraq	Bahrain	12
Al-Ahly	Egypt	11
Olympiakos	Greece	11
CSKA Sofia	Bulgaria	10
Dynamo Kiev	Ukraine	10
Levski Sofia	Bulgaria	10

❀ BRITISH CUP-WINNERS' CUP ❀

Rangers played Newcastle United twice in September 1932. On 14 September 1932, Rangers won 4–1 at Ibrox and, a week later, they lost 5–0 at St James' Park. The games were an unofficial British Cup-Winners' Cup challenge.

❀ A FIRST DOUBLE ❀

In the 1975–76 season, Davie Cooper helped Clydebank to win the Scottish Second Division championship and, in the following season, Clydebank finished runners-up to St Mirren in the Scottish First Division. "The Bankies" thus became the first Scottish team to be promoted in successive seasons.

[†]Apart from Rangers and Celtic (seven-time champions), only Aberdeen (winners in 1980, 1984 and 1985) and Dundee United (1983) have won the Scottish Premier Division.

✳ MARK HATELEY ✳

Mark Hateley was born on 7 November 1961 and began his career at Coventry City, where he played 93 league games for the club between 1978 and 1983 and scored 25 goals. He was transferred to Portsmouth on 6 June 1983 and scored 22 times in his 38 league games. His goalscoring feats for the south coast club attracted Italian giants AC Milan, who paid £1 million to bring him to Serie A. Mark then spent four successful seasons at AC Milan and when he left in 1988, he moved to AS Monaco in the French league.

Hateley joined Rangers from Monaco, signing on 19 July 1990 but, despite scoring on his debut – a 3–1 home win over Dunfermline Athletic on 25 August 1990 – many Rangers fans questioned his ability. At the end of his first season at Ibrox, "Attila", as he was affectionately nicknamed by the Rangers faithful, had helped Rangers to retain the Scottish League championship and his ten goals in 33 league outings were instrumental in doing so. The following season, Mark scored 21 league goals in only 30 games to ensure that the Scottish League championship trophy remained at Ibrox. The 1992–93 season was one of Attila's best ever because not only did he win his third consecutive Scottish League championship-winners' medal but he was also outstanding in the club's ten-match unbeaten run in the Champions League, which saw them exit the competition just one game away from the final. In the "Battle of Britain" game against the English League champions Leeds United, he scored a superb 25-yard left-foot volley before setting up his striking partner, Ally McCoist, for a memorable 2–1 win.

In the 1993–94 season, Hateley lived up to his nickname of "Attila" once again, as he terrorized opponents' defences. In 42 league games, he bagged 22 goals to help Rangers to the Scottish League championship. He left Rangers at the end of the following campaign and joined his former Ibrox team-mate Ray Wilkins at Queens Park Rangers in a deal worth £1.5 million.

During his Ibrox career, Mark scored 115 goals in 222 games for Rangers, won five Scottish Premier League championship titles, two Scottish Cups and three Scottish League Cups. He also won 32 international caps for England, but only one of those caps came during his Ibrox days.

Did You Know That?
At the end of the 1993–94 season, the Scottish Football Writers' Association named Mark their Player of the Year; he was the first Englishman to win the prestigious award.

❊ WIT AND WISDOM OF THE BLUES (16) ❊

"He's got more skill than I had when I was five – in fact he probably has more skill than I have now."
Colin Hendry, on his young son Kyle

❊ AWAY-GOALS EUROPEAN EXITS ❊

Rangers have lost six European ties on the away-goals rule:
Champions League, second round, 2005–06
Rangers v. Villareal (SPA), 2–2 and 1–1
(Villareal won on the away-goals rule)
UEFA Cup, first round, 2002–03
Viktoria Zizkov (CZE) v. Rangers, 2–0 and 1–3
(Viktoria Zizkov won on the away-goals rule)
European Cup, first round, 1993–94
Rangers v. Levski Sofia (BUL), 3–2 and 1–2
(Levski Sofia won on the away-goals rule)
European Cup, first round, 1991–92
Sparta Prague (CZE) v. Rangers, 1–0 and 1–2 (aet)
(Sparta Prague won on the away-goals rule)
UEFA Cup, third round, 1986–87
Rangers v. Borussia Moenchengladbach (GER), 1–1 and 0–0
(Borussia Moenchengladbach won on the away-goals rule)
European Cup-Winners' Cup, second round, 1983–84
Rangers v. FC Porto (POR), 2–1 and 0–1
(FC Porto won on the away-goals rule)

❊ RANGERS PLAYER KISSES MARADONA ❊

Claudio Caniggia made 50 appearances for Rangers from 2001–03 and scored 13 goals. Diego Maradona is one of Caniggia's best friends and the duo once celebrated a goal for Argentina by kissing each other on the lips. When Caniggia's wife, the model Mariana Nannis, was asked what she thought about the incident she said: "At times I believe Diego is in love with my husband. It must be the long hair and big muscles."

❊ AUSTRIA'S CELTIC VISIT IBROX ❊

On 21 January 1933, Austria's Rapid Vienna became the first foreign team to visit Ibrox and a 56,000 crowd were entertained by a scintillating 3–3 draw, with Smith (two) and McPhail scoring for Rangers. Rapid's home colours are green-and-white hooped shirt, green shorts and green socks.

❋ RANGERS UNITED ❋

In the 2003–04 season, Rangers met Manchester United twice in the Champions League. Rangers lost both games, 1–0 at Ibrox and 3–0 at Old Trafford.

❋ RANGERS' FIRST HOME ❋

When Rangers were formed in 1873 their first home was "Fleshers' Haugh", which was owned by the Incorporation of Fleshers (butchers). Rangers played their home games there for two years before moving to various locations, and eventually ending up at their current home, Ibrox, in 1899.

❋ JERUSALEM BEATS RANGERS KEEPER ❋

On 9 May 1937, Scotland played Austria in a friendly at the Praterstadion in Vienna. Rangers captain James McMillan Simpson captained Scotland in the game that ended 1–1, with the Rangers goalkeeper, James Dawson, conceding a goal to Austria's Jerusalem.

❋ THE TROPHY COLLECTOR ❋

During his time with Liverpool, former Rangers manager Graeme Souness had won just about everything going including: five First Division championships (1978–79, 1979–80, 1981–82, 1982–83 and 1983–84), one FA Cup 1992 (as manager), four League Cups (1981, 1982, 1983 and 1984), three European Cups (1978, 1981 and 1984) and three Charity Shields (1979, 1980 and 1982). He played 358 times for the Reds and scored 56 goals.

❋ BATTLE OF BRITAIN ❋

Rangers have met an English team on at least two occasions in all three major European competitions:

Season	Opponent	Comp	Home	Away
2003–04	Manchester United	UCL	0–1	0–3
1992–93	Leeds United	EC	2–1	2–1
1968–69	Newcastle United	ICFC	0–0	0–2
1967–68	Leeds United	ICFC	0–0	0–2
1960–61	Wolverhampton Wanderers	ECWC	2–0	1–1
1962–63	Tottenham Hotspur	ECWC	2–3	2–5

❈ RANGERS XI OF THE 1980s ❈

1
Chris
WOODS

2
Gary
STEVENS

3
Stuart
MUNRO

4
Graham
ROBERTS

5
Terry
BUTCHER

6
Ian
FERGUSON

7
Ray
WILKINS

8
Mark
WALTERS

9
Ally
McCOIST

10
Robert
FLECK

11
Davie
COOPER

Reserves
Nicky *WALKER* • Jimmy *NICHOLL* • Trevor *FRANCIS*
Trevor *STEVEN* • Maurice *JOHNSTON*
Manager
Graeme *SOUNESS*

Did You Know That?
During the 1983–84 pre-season, Rangers signed Ally McCoist from
Sunderland for £185,000, one of the greatest bargain buys the club
has ever made.

❈ TRUE BLUE ❈

In 1922, Jock Buchanan[†] played up front for Greenock Morton when
they caused an upset by beating Rangers 1–0 in the Scottish Cup
final. Then, in December 1927, he joined Rangers, who were the
dominant force in Scottish football at the time. Jock went on to win
four consecutive Scottish League championships (1927–28, 1928–29,
1929–30 and 1930–31) and two Scottish Cups in 1928 and 1930.

*[†] In the 1929 Scottish Cup final, Buchanan was sent off in the 2–0 defeat by Kilmarnock at
Hampden Park. Prior to the start of the 1931–32 season, he moved to Linfield, winning another
league medal and reaching the Irish Cup final, and then played one final season with East
Stirlingshire before his retirement in 1933.*

❀ PFA YOUNG PLAYER OF THE YEAR AWARD ❀

The following Rangers young guns received the award: John MacDonald (1980), Robert Fleck (1987), Charlie Miller (1995), Barry Ferguson (1999) and Kenny Miller (2000).

❀ 100 UP FOR RANGERS ❀

The 2000 Scottish Cup final saw Rangers notch up their 100th competitive trophy success.

❀ RANGERS RESTORE SPANISH RELATIONS ❀

At the start of the 1974–75 season, Rangers were invited by Barcelona to participate in the "Juan Gamper Tournament" at Estadio Camp Nou. Rangers beat Athletic Bilbao 1–0, but then lost 4–1 to the hosts in the final. Rangers had gone a long way in restoring relations between the two teams following the pitch invasion by a section of the Rangers fans after their 1972 European Cup-Winners' Cup triumph over Dynamo Moscow, which had also been played in the Nou Camp.

❀ FIRST SUNDAY GAME ❀

Rangers played their first Sunday game on 17 February 1974 when Dundee were defeated 3–0 at Ibrox in the Scottish Cup. Sunday games were encouraged by the Scottish FA at a time when miners were on strike – a three-day week was in operation and the use of floodlights had been banned to save energy.

❀ FRENCH MASTER CLASS ❀

Mark Hateley played for AS Monaco between 1988 and 1990 and was in the same side as Glenn Hoddle. The Monaco manager at the time was none other than Arsene Wenger.

❀ A HISTORIC INTERNATIONAL ❀

Rangers captain David Meiklejohn led the Scotland team that drew 2–2 with Austria at Hampden Park on 29 November 1933. The match was notable because it was the first time that a continental team had played an international in Scotland. Rangers' George Brown and Bobby McPhail also lined up for Scotland that day.

❀ WE ARE THE CHAMPIONS (10) ❀

Rangers won the 1988–89 Scottish Premier League with 56 points, six clear of Aberdeen who finished as runners-up. In the first Old Firm league game of the season, Graeme Souness's men hammered Celtic 5–1, with Terry Butcher's return to the side after a broken leg adding extra steel to the defence. In total, Rangers – who won 14 of their last 17 league games – won 26, drew four and lost six of their league games, scoring 62 goals and conceding 26. After beating Aberdeen 3–2 in the Scottish League Cup final, Rangers narrowly missed out on the Treble when they lost 1–0 to Celtic in the Scottish Cup final.

Scottish League Premier Division
1988–89

		P	W	D	L	F	A	W	D	L	F	A	Pts
1.	Rangers	36	15	1	2	39	11	11	3	4	23	15	56
2.	Aberdeen	36	10	7	1	26	10	8	7	3	25	15	50
3.	Celtic	36	13	1	4	35	18	8	3	7	31	26	46
4.	Dundee United	36	6	8	4	20	16	10	4	4	24	10	44
5.	Hibernian	36	8	4	6	20	16	5	5	8	17	20	35
6.	Heart of Midlothian	36	7	6	5	22	17	2	7	9	13	25	31
7.	St Mirren	36	5	6	7	17	19	6	1	11	22	36	29
8.	Dundee	36	8	4	6	22	21	1	6	11	12	27	28
9.	Motherwell	36	5	7	6	21	21	2	6	10	14	23	27
10.	Hamilton Academical	36	5	0	13	9	42	1	2	15	10	34	14

❀ WIT AND WISDOM OF THE BLUES (17) ❀

"One of the best years of my life was the very last one of my career. Playing for Rangers was my dream and it meant everything to my family."
Andy Gray

❀ ATTILA'S CLUBS ❀

Rangers legend Mark Hateley, nicknamed "Attila", played for the following clubs during his career: Ross County, Hull City, Queens Park Rangers, Glasgow Rangers, AS Monaco, AC Milan, Portsmouth, Coventry City and Leeds United (on loan). Mark also played for England.

❊ THE EUROPEAN SUPER CUP ❊

The European Super Cup[†] was created in 1972 by a Dutch reporter called Anton Witkamp, who wanted the all-conquering Dutch team at the time, Ajax, to be tested further by other teams in Europe. However, his idea was rejected by the president of UEFA because of a one-year UEFA ban that had been handed out to Rangers, the 1972 European Cup-Winners' Cup winners, following crowd trouble at the 1972 final in Barcelona. Witkamp turned to the Dutch newspaper *De Telegraaf*, who agreed to sponsor the first unofficial European Super Cup won 6–3 on aggregate by Ajax over two legs. Since 1973, UEFA has officially recognized the European Super Cup and, since 1998, it has been a one-off final played in AS Monaco's Stade Louis II. Since 1999, the match has been contested between the European Cup (Champions League) winners and the UEFA Cup winners.

❊ PAST MANAGERS ❊

When Paul LeGuen takes charge of Rangers at the beginning of the 2006–07 season, he will be the 12th manager at the club. These are the 11 men who preceded him and their terms at the helm.

William Wilton	1899–1920
Bill Struth	1920–54
Scot Symon	1954–67
David White	1967–69
William Waddell	1969–72
Jock Wallace	1972–78 and 1983–86
John Greig	1978–83
Graeme Souness	1986–91
Walter Smith	1991–98
Dick Advocaat	1998–2002
Alex McLeish	2002–06

❊ DOUBLE DEBUT DELIGHT ❊

Rangers players Kris Boyd and Chris Burke made their full Scottish international debuts in the Kirin Cup against Bulgaria in Japan on 11 May 2006. Boyd scored twice in the first half, while Burke, a second-half substitute, added two more in the 5–1 victory.

[†]*The European Super Cup was not held in 1981 because European Cup winners, Liverpool, could not agree on a suitable date to play Dynamo Tbilisi, the European Cup-Winners' Cup winners.*

❋ TREBLE-WINNING CAPTAINS ❋

1949	Jock Shaw
1964	Bobby Shearer
1976	John Greig
1978	John Greig
1993	Richard Gough
1999	Lorenzo Amoruso
2003	Barry Ferguson

❋ BACK HOME ❋

After failing to win a third consecutive Scottish First Division championship in the 1921–22 season, Rangers bounced back in the following season[†] to bring the title back to Ibrox.

❋ MONEY BAGS ❋

At the end of the 1893–94 season, Rangers treasurer John Marr announced that the club had quadrupled its income over the previous five years from £1,240 to £5,227.

❋ MR RELIABLE ❋

Sandy Jardine played in all three of Scotland's games during the 1974 World Cup finals but, despite the fact that Scotland did not lose a game, they still went out of the competition on goal difference. Jardine would go on to represent his country in the 1978 World Cup finals in Argentina. All 38 of his Scottish caps were won during his Ibrox days.

❋ THE LAST ACT ❋

After 17 seasons at the club, John Greig played his last game for Rangers in the 1978 Scottish Cup final. It was a victorious send-off, as Rangers beat Aberdeen 2–1 to hand Greig his sixth winners' medal in the competition. Just short of his 35th birthday, John's last act in a Rangers shirt was to hold aloft a trophy – a fitting tribute to a true Rangers legend. Shortly after retiring as a player John was appointed manager of Rangers.

[†]*During the 1922–23 season, three clubs in the Scottish Second Division (Cowdenbeath, St Bernard's and St Johnstone) all had points deducted for using ineligible players.*

❊ SANDY JARDINE ❊

William Pullar "Sandy" Jardine was born in Edinburgh on 31 December 1948 and joined Rangers from school at just 15 years of age. He made his debut for Rangers in February 1967 in a 5–1 home win over Hearts. Sandy had been brought into the side following the humiliating loss to Berwick Rangers in the Scottish Cup the week before, but played well enough to retain his place in the side for the remainder of the season.

In May 1967, Sandy played for Rangers in the European Cup-Winners' Cup final against Bayern Munich, but sadly the men from Ibrox lost the game 0–1. In the final, Jardine's opposite No. 4 was the magnificent Franz Beckenbauer, who spoke very highly of Sandy's performance after the game. Throughout the 1967–68 season, Sandy was a regular in the Rangers team that finished runners-up in the championship to Celtic for the third consecutive season.

At the beginning of the 1968–69 season, Rangers manager Davie White switched Sandy to centre-forward. Amazingly, Sandy scored 11 goals in 12 consecutive starts at centre-forward. However, once again Rangers found themselves runners-up to Celtic in the league. The following season was no better, although one major change to Sandy's playing career occurred when Willie Waddell, who had replaced Davie White as manager, switched Sandy to full-back for the last three games of the season. Sandy was a tough, but fair, tackler and had an appetite to attack from his defensive position. The move proved a masterstroke, as Sandy became one of the game's first, and best, overlapping attacking full-backs.

In 1970, Sandy won his first medal with Rangers when they defeated Celtic 1–0 in the Scottish League Cup final. Then, on 11 November 1970, Sandy won the first of his 38 international caps for Scotland when he came on as a substitute in a 1–0 win over Denmark at Hampden Park. Sandy was a key member of Rangers' 1972 European Cup-Winners' Cup-winning team, playing in every round – indeed, between 27 April 1972 and 30 August 1975 he did not miss a single game for the club (171). In 1973, Sandy won his first Scottish FA Cup-winners' medal, as Rangers beat Celtic 3–2 in the final. However, even more success was to come, as Sandy won two Trebles with Rangers in 1975–76 and 1977–78. His winners' medal haul with Rangers includes three championships, five Scottish Cups, five Scottish League Cups and one European Cup-Winners' Cup. After 674 appearances and 77 goals for Rangers, Sandy joined Hearts in 1982 and helped his hometown club finish runners-up in both the league and Scottish Cup in 1985–86.

❊ RANGERS MANAGERS XI ❊

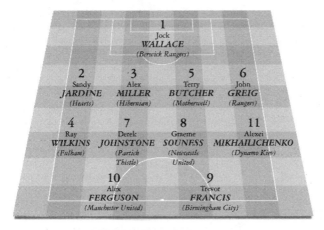

1
Jock
WALLACE
(Berwick Rangers)

2
Sandy
JARDINE
(Hearts)

3
Alex
MILLER
(Hibernian)

5
Terry
BUTCHER
(Motherwell)

6
John
GREIG
(Rangers)

4
Ray
WILKINS
(Fulham)

7
Derek
JOHNSTONE
(Partick Thistle)

8
Graeme
SOUNESS
(Newcastle United)

11
Alexei
MIKHAILICHENKO
(Dynamo Kiev)

10
Alex
FERGUSON
(Manchester United)

9
Trevor
FRANCIS
(Birmingham City)

Substitutes
Bobby **BROWN** *(Sunderland & Scotland)* • Paul **GASCOIGNE** *(Kettering Town)*
Graham **ROBERTS**[†] *(Clyde)* • Mark **HATELEY** *(Hull City)*
Colin **HENDRIE** *(Blackpool)*
Manager
William **WADDELL** *(Kilmarnock)*

❊ RED LICHTIES STUN 'GERS ❊

In the 1973–74 season, Arbroath beat Rangers 3–2 at Ibrox to record their first ever away win in the league over Rangers.

❊ A LANDMARK SEASON FOR COOPER ❊

The 1982–83 season saw two significant landmarks in the Rangers career of Davie Cooper: he scored his first hat-trick for Rangers in a League Cup tie against Kilmarnock and scored his first, and only, European goal, for the club against Borussia Dortmund in a UEFA Cup tie at Ibrox. This season was also Davie's most prolific goalscoring season for the club, as he found the net 12 times in all competitions.

'On 17 October 1987, Rangers goalkeeper Chris Woods was sent off in the Old Firm game at Ibrox. Defender Graham Roberts – a fellow England international – took over in goal. The match ended in a 2–2 draw.

❋ WIT AND WISDOM OF THE BLUES (18) ❋

"We set realistic targets, but when you are at Rangers it is the championship which really matters and rightly so. I felt at the start of the season we have the players to push Celtic and we did exactly that."
***Alex McLeish**, on his Treble-winning squad*

❋ RANGERS TV ❋

Rangers TV is operated by the Irish sports broadcaster Setanta and, for a £14-per-month Sky package, fans receive live coverage of all Scottish Premiership games. The same package costs £6.99 a month on ntl:home, which hosts a daily news show and a phone-in.

❋ BIRTH OF THE SCOTTISH LEAGUE ❋

In March 1890, Renton FC invited 13 other clubs to attend a meeting to discuss the formation of a Scottish League. The clubs invited were Abercorn, Cambuslang, Celtic, Clyde, Cowlairs, Dumbarton, Heart of Midlothian, Queen's Park, Rangers, St Bernard's, St Mirren, Third Lanark, Vale of Leven and, of course, Renton. The Scottish League was inaugurated in April 1890, without Clyde and Queen's Park, who declined to attend the meeting, and St Bernard's, who were not elected.

❋ ALCOHOL BAN ❋

When Rangers signed a new sponsorship deal with the brewery Carling, a number of Rangers' Muslim fans called upon the club to remove the logo from their shirts as their religion forbade them from wearing anything associated with promoting alcohol. Rangers duly obliged and now sell an unbranded shirt especially for their Muslim following. To date, Celtic have not followed suit.

❋ RANGERS OFF THE HOOK ❋

In 1884, Arbroath[†] beat Rangers 4–3 at Gayfield in a Scottish Cup match. However, when Rangers complained that the pitch wasn't wide enough, the SFA ordered a replay, which Rangers won 8–1.

[†]On 12 September 1885, Arbroath, known as the "Red Lichties", beat Bon Accord 36–0 in a Scottish Cup first-round tie. The result is a world record score for a cup-tie and Jocky Petrie's 13 goals in the game is also a record that remains unequalled.

❉ UP FOR THE CUP (11) ❉

It had been 11 years since Rangers had won the Scottish Cup, but that particular bogey was put to bed in the 1991–92 season. In the third round, Rangers beat Aberdeen 1–0 at Pittodrie and in the fourth round, played at Ibrox, Rangers saw off holders Motherwell with a 2–1 victory. The quarter-finals saw Rangers beat St Johnstone 3–0 away with Ally McCoist scoring against his old club. The semi-final was an Old Firm encounter at Hampden Park, which was settled by an Ally McCoist goal. Rangers beat Airdrieonians 2–1 in a disappointing final at Hampden Park.

SCOTTISH FA CUP FINAL
9 MAY 1992, HAMPDEN PARK, GLASGOW
Rangers (2) 2   v.   Airdrieonians (0) 1
(Hateley, McCoist)   (Smith)
Att. 44,045
Rangers: Andy Goram, Gary Stevens, Davie Robertson, Richard Gough, Nigel Spackman, John Brown, Ian Durrant, Stuart McCall, Ally McCoist, Mark Hateley, Alexei Mikhailichenko.
Sub: Dale Gordon.

Did You Know That?
In the 1991–92 season, Rangers won their fourth successive Scottish Premier League title in Walter Smith's first full season in charge. In doing so, the team scored more than 100 goals (101) for the first time since the Scottish Premier League began, in 1975–76.

❉ RECORD AWAY CROWD FOR MORTON ❉

Greenock Morton achieved their record away crowd when 112,500 fans turned up to see their 1964 Scottish League Cup final against Rangers at Hampden Park. Their vast travelling support would have gone home disappointed, however, as Rangers won 5–0.

❉ LES VERTS DEFEAT LES BLEUS ❉

In the 1975–76 European Cup – with the final scheduled for Hampden Park – Rangers lost to the French side St Etienne, in the second round. Rangers won the home leg 2–1, but were beaten 2–0 by "Les Verts" ("The Greens"), in the Stade Geoffroy-Guichard. St Etienne went all the way to the final of the competition that year, but Bayern Munich defeated them.

❋ THE DUTCH MASTER ❋

In 1999, Rangers signed Michael Mols – a product of the famous youth system at Ajax – for a fee of £4 million from the Dutch side FC Twente. Mols scored two goals on his debut, away to FA Haka (Finland), and scored a total of five goals in his first two games for Rangers. However, shortly after his arrival at the club, he got injured in a Champions League game against Bayern Munich and the resulting operation ruled him out of action until August 2000. When he returned to first-team action he was as good as ever and scored many decisive goals in Rangers' 2002–03 championship-winning season. He left Rangers in 2004 and joined Dutch side FC Utrecht.

❋ PRINCE OF ORANGE ❋

Frank de Boer, a Rangers player from January to May 2004, is the most capped player in the history of Dutch football, having played for his country 112 times.

❋ SPEED MACHINE ❋

In July 1998, Rangers signed Andrei Kanchelskis[†] from Fiorentina for £5.5 million and the Russian made his debut against Shelbourne in the UEFA Cup. Kanchelskis had been a key member of the Manchester United side that won the club's first domestic Double in the 1993–94 season. Andrei played 75 league games for Rangers (11 as a substitute) and scored 11 goals. On the 30 August 2002, Andrei joined Southampton on a free transfer following a loan spell with Manchester City.

❋ BANNED FOR RECEIVING £1 ❋

In December 1887, Rangers forward Bob Brand was banned by the Scottish Football Association for two months after they found him guilty of accepting £1 from Hearts to play for them in a match in August 1887, shortly before he transferred to Rangers from Queen of the South Wanderers. This was at a time when players were not professionals and were not permitted to accept payments for playing.

[†]Andrei Kanchelskis became only the second player to be sent off in a Wembley cup final when he handled a shot on the line when playing for Manchester United against Aston Villa in the 1994 League Cup final.

❉ COOPER'S EARLY YEARS ❉

When he was young boy, Davie Cooper was an avid Rangers supporter and, when he was not playing himself, he used to go to Ibrox with his father and brother. Davie's first team was the local juvenile side Udston United. He then moved on to Hamilton Avondale and played with the Under-16 team before progressing to the Under-18s. When he was with Hamilton Avondale, he was working as an apprentice printer with the brothers who ran the club. He then signed as a professional for Clydebank in 1974 before going on to join Rangers in 1977.

❉ BARKER OFF TO A FLYER ❉

John Bell Barker joined Rangers from Linthouse in 1892 and made an immediate impact, scoring five goals in his first three matches. On 18 March 1893, he made his international debut for Scotland and hit a first-half hat-trick in an 8–0 win over Wales at Action Park, Wrexham.

❉ EUROPEAN PENALTY SHOOT-OUT FIRST ❉

In the 2001–02 season, Rangers won their first ever penalty shoot-out in European competition when they beat Paris Saint-Germain 4–3 on penalties in the third round of the UEFA Cup after the two sides has played out two goalless draws.

❉ LEAGUE CUP RECORD SCORE ❉

Rangers annihilated Ayr United 7–0 in the semi-final of the Scottish League Cup at Hampden Park on 8 April 2000. The score was an all-time club record in the competition.

❉ RANGERS LOSE A LEGEND ❉

On Wednesday, 22 March 1995, Davie Cooper and the former Celtic striker, Charlie Nicholas, were recording a coaching film for young children at Broadwood Stadium. Davie collapsed during filming after suffering a brain haemorrhage and subsequently died. His funeral took place at Hillhouse Parish Church, Hamilton, on 27 March 1995, and in his moving eulogy to Davie, the Rangers manager Walter Smith said: "God gave Davie Cooper a talent. He would not be disappointed with how it was used."

❊ RANGERS XI OF THE 1990s ❊

1
Andy
GORAM

2
Sergio
PORRINI

3
Richard
GOUGH

4
Allan
McLAREN

5
John
BROWN

6
Rino
GATTUSO

7
Ian
DURRANT

8
Jorg
ALBERTZ

9
Paul
GASCOIGNE

10
Mark
HATELEY

11
Brain
LAUDRUP

Reserves
Anti *NIEMI* • Colin *HENDRIE* • Terry *HURLOCK*
Stuart *MCCALL* • Gordon *DURIE*
Manager
Walter *SMITH*

Did You Know That?
When Rangers lost 2–1 at Hibernian on 12 October 1996 in the Scottish Premier League, Brian Laudrup missed two penalties.

❊ RED MACHINE HALTED BY RANGERS ❊

Rangers began their 1987–88 European Cup campaign with a tricky tie against the Ukrainian (then Russian) champions, Dynamo Kiev. Rangers lost the first leg 0–1 in the Ukraine, but progressed to the second round following a 2–0 win at Ibrox in the second leg.

❊ RANGERS VISIT HELL IN THE HOLY CITY ❊

On 15 September 1998, Rangers visited the holy city of Jerusalem to play Beitar Jerusalem Football Club in a UEFA Cup, first-round, first-leg tie. Rangers managed a 1–1 draw in the Teddy Kollek Memorial Stadium, nicknamed "Gehinnom" (Hell), because of the hostile atmosphere the home fans generate when opposing teams visit it.

❋ AN ENGLISHMAN IN GLASGOW ❋

Rangers were in the midst of an Anglo revolution when Gary Stevens joined them from Everton for £1.25 million in the summer of 1988. Manager Graeme Souness was unashamedly buying non-Scottish players to bolster his side. Stevens' first season at Ibrox ended with a Scottish Premier Division title. He went on to win five more league championship-winners' medals, two Scottish Cups and three Scottish League Cups.

❋ RANGERS 6 RAITH ROVERS 6 ❋

During Rangers' 1958–59 championship-winning season, they drew 2–2 with Raith Rovers[†] at Stark's Park and in the return game at Ibrox the match finished 4–4.

❋ HISTORIC VICTORY IN OLD FIRM GAME ❋

On Sunday, 2 May 1999, Rangers created history by winning the Scottish Premier League championship at Celtic Park in a rampaging Old Firm game in which referee Hugh Dallas was injured by a coin thrown from the crowd. The match was only 22 seconds old before the first foul was committed, with a second foul following before the minute was up. Celtic's Stephane Mahe was the first player to receive his marching orders, sent off midway through the first half. Neil McCann, who had scored the goal that separated the two teams at the interval, scored once again after the break as Rangers romped to a 3–0 win over their archrivals with Jorg Albertz scoring Rangers' other goal – from a controversial penalty awarded just minutes after Dallas had received treatment for his wounds.

The referee, now swathed in bandages, had spoken to both teams at half-time, demanding a less tempestuous second 45 minutes but, although the second half was played in a calmer atmosphere, two more players were sent off. Rod Wallace was given his marching orders in the final ten minutes, followed by Celtic's Vidar Riseth.

At the final whistle, the Rangers players went to the goal where their fans were congregated to celebrate, but a barrage of missiles from either side hastened their retreat to the dressing room. It was Rangers' first championship-clinching win at Celtic Park.

[†] *In 1923, the Raith Rovers team was shipwrecked when their boat ran aground on their way to playing several friendly matches on the Canary Islands. Thankfully, all the players disembarked safely and continued on their journey a few days later.*

❉ WE ARE THE CHAMPIONS (11) ❉

Walter Smith strengthened his team at the beginning of the 1996–97 season for an all-out assault on a ninth successive championship title. Players such as Jorg Albertz and Joachim Bjorkland added the desired strength and Rangers got off to a flyer, winning their opening seven games, culminating in a 2–0 Old Firm win at Ibrox. Hibernian brought Rangers' progress to a slight halt in the eighth game of the season, winning 2–1 at Easter Road, but the Ibrox men still went on to win the championship – their ninth in a row – in the penultimate game of the season, following a 1–0 away victory over Dundee United. Rangers also collected the Scottish League Cup that season, beating Hearts 4–3 in the final.

Tennents Scottish League Premier Division
1996–97

	P	W	D	L	F	A	W	D	L	F	A	Pts
1. **Rangers**	36	13	2	3	44	16	12	3	3	41	17	80
2. Celtic	36	14	2	2	48	9	9	4	5	30	23	75
3. Dundee United	36	10	4	4	21	10	7	5	6	25	23	60
4. Heart of Midlothian	36	8	6	4	27	20	6	4	8	19	23	52
5. Dunfermline Athletic	36	8	4	6	32	30	4	5	9	20	35	45
6. Aberdeen	36	6	8	4	25	19	4	6	8	20	35	44
7. Kilmarnock	36	8	4	6	28	26	3	2	13	13	35	39
8. Motherwell	36	5	5	8	24	25	4	6	8	20	30	38
9. Hibernian	36	6	4	8	18	25	3	7	8	20	30	38
10. Raith Rovers	36	3	5	10	18	39	3	2	13	11	34	25

❉ PRELIMINARY ROUND EXIT ❉

AEK Athens knocked Rangers out of the 1994–95 Champions League at the preliminary round hurdle. Rangers lost the two-leg tie 3–0 on aggregate.

❉ BIG ECK'S FIRST DOMESTIC CUP DEFEAT ❉

Rangers' 4–3 penalty shoot-out defeat by Hibernian, following a 1–1 draw at Hampden Park, in the Scottish League Cup semi-final on 5 February 2004, was the first time that Alex McLeish had lost a domestic cup-tie since taking over as Rangers manager in December 2001.

❊ GREEN AND BLUE MOJO ❊

Striker Mo Johnston[†] was a prolific goalscorer everywhere he played:

Partick Thistle	41 goals	85 games	1981–83
Watford	23 goals	38 games	1983–84
Celtic	55 goals	99 games	1984–87
Nantes	22 goals	66 game	1987–90
Rangers	31 goals	76 games	1990–93
Everton	10 goals	34 games	1993–94
Hearts	5 goals	35 games	1994–95
Falkirk	1 goal	10 games	1985–96
Kansas City Wizards	30 goals	138 games	1996–2001
Scotland	13 goals	37 games	1984–92

❊ THE SCOTTISH FWA AWARD ❊

This is the main award presented by the Scottish Football Writers' Association. The following Rangers players have won it: John Greig (1966 and 1976), Dave Smith (1972), Sandy Jardine (1975), Derek Johnstone (1978), Richard Gough (1989), Ally McCoist (1992), Andy Goram (1993), Mark Hateley (1994), Brian Laudrup (1995 and 1997), Paul Gascoigne (1996) and Barry Ferguson (2000 and 2003).

❊ JOHN GREIG – GREATEST RANGER EVER ❊

At an awards ceremony in Glasgow on 21 March 1999, John Greig was voted "The Greatest Ranger Ever". After receiving his prestigious award, Greig cast his mind back to the 1971 Ibrox Disaster and said: "The disaster will never leave me. Never a day goes by that it doesn't go through my mind. I still get letters from guys who have never been back to Ibrox for a game since that day. I have taken some of them around the stadium for them to see what it is like now. The new stadium is, in fact, a testament to those who died. In the trophy room, there is a beautiful picture of the old stadium up on the wall. For me, it is one of the most important things in that room and I make a point of showing it to the people who go there. It's important, especially for the young fans who have only seen the new stadium, that they know the history of this club, where we came from and why we came from that point."

[†]In 1984, Mo Johnston became the most expensive striker in Scottish football when Celtic paid Watford £400,000 for his services.

❋ RECORD NUMBER OF LOONS ❋

In 1970, the record home attendance for Station Park was set when Rangers played Forfar Athletic there in front of 10,780 fans. Forfar Athletic are nicknamed "The Loons".

❋ ENGLISH MINNOWS DUMP BLUES ❋

In the 1966–67 season, Rangers were humiliated in the Scottish Cup, losing 0–1 to Berwick Rangers[†].

❋ HEY BIG SPENDERS ❋

In October 1968, Rangers broke the Scottish transfer record by signing Colin Stein from Hibernian for £100,000.

❋ BLUES DECIDE TO CHANGE "COLOURS" ❋

On 1 October 1976, Rangers announced that they would start signing players regardless of their religion.

❋ LUCKY 13 ❋

Rangers boasted 13 international players in their championship-winning side of 1932–33. Ten were Scottish internationals and the other three were Irish internationals.

❋ A DOSE OF "M AND B" ❋

During the 1960s, the Rangers pair of Jimmy Millar and Ralph Brand were known as "A dose of M and B".

❋ TWO 'GERS BEAT WORLD CHAMPIONS ❋

On 15 April 1967, Scotland visited Wembley to play England in a Home International and European Championship group eight game. England had not been beaten since winning the World Cup final against West Germany in the same stadium nine months earlier. Two Rangers players, John Greig and Ronnie McKinnon, were in the Scotland team that beat the world champions 3–2 that day.

[†]*Although Berwick Rangers play in the Scottish League, they play their home games at Shielfield Park, Tweedmouth, Berwick-upon-Tweed, in England.*

❈ FIVE FROM 11 ❈

Of the 11 clubs that formed the original Scottish League in 1891–92, only five still play in the Scottish League:

Rangers ❖ Celtic ❖ Dumbarton ❖ Hearts ❖ St Mirren

❈ LATE MAIL ❈

The SFA prevented Rangers from participating in the first Scottish FA Cup competition in 1873–74 because their entry form had arrived at SFA headquarters too late.

❈ RANGERS' ENGLISH FA CUP WITHDRAWAL ❈

Rangers entered the English FA Cup in 1885 but elected not to play in the competition rather than to play their cup-tie against a professional club, Rawtenstall.

❈ YOUNG GOALKEEPER ❈

Rangers completed the Double in 1952–53 despite having to place their defender George Young in goal for 20 minutes in the Scottish Cup final against Aberdeen.

❈ THE FIRST SCOTTISH TREBLE ❈

In the 1948–49[†] season, Rangers became the first club in Scotland to win the domestic Treble. Rangers beat Raith Rovers 2–0 in the Scottish League Cup final at Hampden Park and, after securing the league title, rounded off their Treble-winning season by beating Clyde 4–0 in the Scottish FA Cup final at Hampden Park.

❈ BARREN SEASON FOR RANGERS ❈

The 1951–52 season was a barren one for Rangers. Hibernian won their fourth league championship, Dundee won their first League Cup (they defeated Rangers 3–2 in the final) and Motherwell lifted the Scottish FA Cup for the first time in the club's history (beating Dundee 4–0 in the final).

[†]*During the 1948–49 season, a rule was introduced whereby obstructing an opponent was deemed an offence that would be penalized by the award of a free-kick.*

✳ UP FOR THE CUP (12) ✳

Rangers had already won the 1999–2000 championship with six games to spare and the only thing stopping them from clinching the Double was a Scottish Cup final encounter with Aberdeen at Hampden Park. Rangers had beaten St Johnstone 2–0 away in the third round followed by a 1–0 win over Morton (played at St Mirren's ground in Paisley) in the fourth round. They then swept aside Hearts in the quarter-finals with a 4–1 win at Ibrox and followed that by slaughtering Ayr United 7–0 in the semi-final at Hampden Park. In the final, goals from Albertz, Dodds, Van Bronckhorst and Vidmar handed Rangers a comfortable 4–0 win and the Double.

SCOTTISH **FA** CUP FINAL
27 MAY 2000, HAMPDEN PARK, GLASGOW
Rangers (1) 4   v.   Aberdeen (0) 0
(Van Bronckhorst, Vidmar,
Dodds, Albertz)
Att. 50,685
Rangers: Stefan Klos, Claudio Reyna, Arthur Numan,
Barry Ferguson, Craig Moore, Tony Vidmar, Andrei Kanchelskis,
Rod Wallace, Billy Dodds, Jorg Albertz,
Giovanni van Bronckhorst.
Subs: Neil McCann, Terimoglu Tugay, Sergio Porini.

Did You Know That?
After Rangers clinched the Scottish Premier League title with victory over St Johnstone, the Rangers manager Dick Advocaat insisted that the players go out that night and celebrate in Perth with the fans.

✳ MR CARING ✳

On 2 January 1971, 66 Rangers fans died in the Ibrox Disaster. It was not until the Monday morning after the game that the Rangers players began to comprehend the full extent of what had occurred. Speaking about the tragic incident, Sandy Jardine, who played in the game, said this about his manager Willie Waddell: "Everyone injured was to receive a visit from a player or an official and the club was to be represented at every funeral. If an injured fan had a favourite player, and word got back to Ibrox, Mr Waddell would make sure that player made a personal visit. We didn't train for two weeks, but no one could say Rangers didn't respond to the tragedy. Waddell was magnificent."

❋ WIT AND WISDOM OF THE BLUES (19) ❋

"Ibrox really is a special place. It's incredible the bond fans have with parts of the ground. They can remember the day Baxter passed from here or there and from where Gazza scored."
Sandy Jardine

❋ MORE CELEBRITY RANGERS FANS ❋

Clive Anderson	*television personality*
"Stone Cold" Steve Austin	*wrestler*
Kenneth Branagh	*actor*
Drew Carey	*actor*
Robert Carlyle	*actor*
Ian McCallum	*author*
Ryan Moloney	*Toadfish in* Neighbours
Arnold Palmer	*golfer*
Gary Player	*golfer*
Jamie Redknapp	*footballer*
Wet Wet Wet	*band*
Kirsty Young	*television newsreader*

❋ RANGERS LIGHT UP LONDON ❋

On 17 October 1951, Rangers travelled to London to play Arsenal at Highbury in a game inaugurating the Gunners' new floodlights. Rangers lost 3–2 in front of 62,000 fans.

❋ THE IRON CURTAIN ❋

Rangers' famous defence from 1946 to 1953, and the foundation for the club's tremendous success during the period, was nicknamed "The Iron Curtain". The unit comprised of six players over the eight years: Bobby Brown, Sammy Cox, Ian McColl, Jock Shaw, Willie Woodburn and George Young.

❋ JAGS DO RANGERS A FAVOUR ❋

On 5 March 1960, Rangers beat Partick Thistle 2–0 in the Scottish Cup semi-final in front of 60,000 fans at Ibrox. Partick, nicknamed "The Jags", had successfully requested that the game be switched from a neutral venue for financial reasons. Rangers went on to lose the final to Morton (1–0).

❄ ALLY McCOIST ❄

Alistair "Ally" Murdoch McCoist was born on 24 September 1962 and grew up in East Kilbride. He began his professional career at St Johnstone and scored 22 goals in 38 outings during the 1980–81 season. His goalscoring exploits for the Saints soon attracted not only the top clubs in Scotland but a few south of the border as well. Rangers were very anxious to sign the young McCoist, but Ally opted to join Sunderland. However, things did not go well for Ally at Roker Park and he scored just eight goals in 56 games before John Greig signed him for Glasgow Rangers in 1983.

After 15 years at Ibrox, Ally had smashed just about every club goalscoring record that existed. Between the 1983–84 and 1997–98 seasons, Ally finished as Rangers' top goalscorer in nine of the 15 seasons in which he he graced the famous blue shirt. He managed to score 34 league goals in a single season on three occasions (1986–87, 1991–92 and 1992–93); he scored 28 hat-tricks for Rangers, including five hat-tricks in two different seasons; and he sits proudly behind Bob Hamilton in the Old Firm goalscoring charts, having scored 27 times against the archrivals (Hamilton hit 35). However, the one record that he wanted above all the others is his: Ally McCoist is Rangers' highest ever goalscorer. He scored 251 league goals and a total of 355 goals in all competitions for Rangers (in a total of 581 games for the club).

Ally simply possessed the knack of being in the right place in the penalty box at the right time and scored a great many of his goals when players surrounded him. He could turn on a sixpence in the box, was as sharp as a razor and had lightning reflexes: he was the ultimate predator in front of goal during his years with Rangers. He won ten Scottish League championship-winners' medals (including nine in a row), one Scottish Cup-winners' medal and nine Scottish League Cup-winners' medals. In 1992 and 1993, his 34 league goals in each of those two seasons would have been enough to win him the European Golden Boot Award but, unfortunately for Ally, the award was suspended during those seasons. In 1992, he won the Scottish PFA Players' Player of the Year and the Scottish Football Writers' Player of the Year. He is Scotland's third highest international goalscorer, with 19 goals in 61 matches (Denis Law and Kenny Dalglish scored 30 each), and is a member of Scotland's Football Hall of Fame.

During the summer of 1998, Ally joined Kilmarnock, where he played for three seasons under Bobby Williamson, before retiring from the game. In 2004, he joined the coaching staff of Scotland's national team under his former manager at Rangers, Walter Smith.

❋ GASCOIGNE PLAYS AN IMAGINARY FLUTE ❋

In January 1998, Paul Gascoigne was fined two weeks' wages by Rangers and was severely reprimanded by the SFA for his flute-playing mime in a match against Celtic. This was the second time that Gascoigne had been in trouble for the provocative anti-Catholic gesture of flute-playing. In 1995, shortly after his transfer to Ibrox from Lazio, he made the same gesture after scoring a goal, apparently having been encouraged to do so by some of his team-mates.

❋ STRANGE BUT TRUE ❋

Five teams have won the European Cup-Winners' Cup despite the fact that they had not won their own domestic cup during the previous season. Fiorentina† won the inaugural European Cup-Winners' Cup in 1960–61 even though they had lost the Italian Cup final in 1960 to Double-winners Juventus. In the 1971–72 season, Rangers were the European Cup-Winners' Cup winners despite having lost the 1971 Scottish FA Cup final to Celtic, the Scottish First Division champions, after a replay. Anderlecht won the competition in 1978 after having lost the 1977 Belgian Cup final to champions FC Brugge. In 1981, Dynamo Tbilisi won the competition even though they had lost the 1980 Soviet Union Cup final to Shakyhtor Donetsk. Finally, Barcelona won the 1997 European Cup-Winners' Cup despite losing the 1996 Copa del Rey to Atletico Madrid, who won the Spanish Double that season.

❋ SCOTTISH PREMIER LEAGUE WINNERS ❋

At the beginning of the 1998–99 season the new Scottish Premier League was established††. Rangers have won four of the eightScottish Premier League championships played for up to the end of the 2005–06 season (in 1999, 2000, 2003 and 2005).

†Both Fiorentina and Anderlecht succumbed to the European Cup-Winners' Cup jinx, whereby no team has ever managed to defend the trophy, even though the defending champions have reached the final the following year on no fewer than eight occasions: Fiorentina, winners in 1961, lost the 1962 final to Atletico Madrid. Anderlecht, winners in 1976, lost the 1977 final to SV Hamburg (they reached the final in 1978 for the third consecutive year where they beat Austria Vienna 4–0 at the Parc des Princes in Paris).

††Apart from Rangers and Celtic (also four-time champions), no other club has won the Scottish Premier League.

❋ DUMBARTON BETTER THE OLD FIRM ❋

Dumbarton were the first club to win back-to-back Scottish First Division championships. In 1890–91, Dumbarton and Rangers shared the first ever Scottish First Division championship and Dumbarton retained the title in 1891–92. Celtic won back-to-back championships in 1892–93 and 1893–94, while Rangers had to wait until 1898–99 and 1899–1900 to achieve the feat.

❋ WEE WILLIE OFF TO A FLYER FOR SCOTLAND ❋

Rangers' Willie Henderson made his debut for Scotland on 20 October 1962, scoring Scotland's winning goal in a 3–2 victory over Wales in their Home Championship encounter at Ninian Park, Cardiff. Eric Caldow, the Rangers and Scotland captain, also scored in the game, from the penalty spot.

❋ THE DRYBOROUGH CUP ❋

The Dryborough[†] Cup, played during the pre-season and a straight knock-out tournament, was held between 1971 and 1980. The entrants were the eight teams that had scored the most Scottish First Division league goals during the previous campaign with the top four clubs being seeded to avoid each other in the first round. When the Scottish Premier Division was established in 1974, the Drybrough Cup was put on hold. It was reintroduced in 1979, with the four highest-scoring teams in the Scottish Premier Division, plus the two highest-scoring teams in the Scottish First and Second Divisions invited. Rangers only won the trophy once, beating Celtic in the 1979 final. Previous winners are:

1971	Aberdeen
1972	Hibernian
1973	Hibernian
1974	Celtic
1975–78	*No competition*
1979	Rangers
1980	Aberdeen

'Drybrough and Co. Ltd's sponsorship of the tournament made it the first ever sponsored football competition exclusively for Scottish clubs. The tournament also afforded the Scottish Football League (SFL) the opportunity to experiment with any new rule changes they had in mind for the game. For example, in the 1973–74 Dryborough Cup, the SFL declared a "no offside" rule and, in another year, they introduced substitute boards.

❊ WE ARE THE CHAMPIONS (12) ❊

The 2004–05 season was a shoot-out between Rangers and Celtic that lasted ten months and which came down to a dramatic final day that was full of twists and turns. On 22 May 2005, Rangers had to travel to Hibernian while Celtic were away to Motherwell. Celtic had 92 points to Rangers' 90, while Hibernian were looking for a single point that would guarantee them third place in the table and secure them a place in the following season's UEFA Cup. Nacho Novo's goal gave Rangers a 1–0 win in Edinburgh and the attention switched to Motherwell, where Celtic were leading 1–0 with only two minutes to play. Amazingly, Motherwell scored twice to hand Rangers their 51st title.

Bank of Scotland Premier League
2004–05

		P	W	D	L	F	A	W	D	L	F	A	Pts
1.	Rangers	38	15	2	2	48	12	14	4	1	30	10	93
2.	Celtic	38	15	0	4	41	15	15	2	2	44	20	92
3.	Hibernian	38	9	4	6	32	26	9	3	7	32	31	61
4.	Aberdeen	38	8	4	6	22	17	10	3	7	22	22	61
5.	Hearts	38	9	4	6	25	15	4	7	8	18	26	50
6.	Motherwell	38	8	4	7	29	22	5	5	9	17	27	48
7.	Kilmarnock	38	10	2	7	32	20	5	2	12	17	35	49
8.	Inverness Cal. Thistle	38	7	4	9	23	24	4	7	7	18	23	44
9.	Dundee United	38	4	7	8	22	28	4	5	10	19	31	36
10.	Livingston	38	5	4	10	22	34	4	4	11	12	27	35
11.	Dunfermline	38	5	9	5	23	19	3	1	15	11	41	34
12.	Dundee	38	7	4	8	21	24	1	5	13	16	47	33

❊ EIGHT BEFORE RANGERS ❊

Eight teams won the Scottish FA Cup before Rangers first picked up the trophy in 1894:

Queen's Park[†] ❖ Vale of Leven ❖ Dumbarton ❖ Renton
Hibernian ❖ Third Lanark ❖ Hearts ❖ Celtic

[†]*In 1873, Queen's Park sent letters to other Scottish clubs asking for a donation of £1 towards purchasing a trophy similar to the English FA Cup that had first been competed for in 1872. As a result, the Scottish FA Cup came into being and is the oldest trophy in the world still in existence, as the English equivalent has been replaced several times over the years.*

❋ TEN-IN-A-ROW BUSTERS ❋

Towards the end of the 1974–75 season, Rangers were on the verge of clinching the Scottish League championship, but their influential captain John Greig was suffering with a recurring hamstring injury at the time. The crunch match came on 29 March 1975, when Rangers faced Hibernian needing only a draw to be crowned champions. Manager Jock Wallace had a word with Greig and decided to put him on the bench in case he was needed; the captain's armband for the game went to Sandy Jardine. With only minutes to go, the scores were level at 1–1 and Wallace sent on an unfit Greig, who fittingly held the championship trophy aloft after the game ended with the scores still at 1–1. In the end, Rangers won the title by a margin of seven points over Hibernian but, more importantly for the club, they prevented Celtic from claiming their tenth consecutive championship. It was Rangers' first title success since the victorious 1963–64 campaign.

❋ A STICKY SITUATION ❋

On 29 October 1886, Rangers travelled up to Liverpool to face Everton (nicknamed "The Toffees") in an English FA Cup first-round game. The night before the game, the hotel's owner asked the entire Rangers team to leave the hotel because they were too noisy. The players and staff packed their bags, found another hotel, and the next day beat Everton 1–0 at Anfield thanks to a Charlie Heggie goal.

❋ SCOTTISH OWN GOAL BLUES ❋

The following Rangers players have all been unlucky enough to score an own goal playing for Scotland:

Player	Opponent	Date	Result
Neilly Gibson	England	6 April 1895	0–3 (l)
Eric Caldow	N. Ireland	5 November 1958	2–2 (d)
Ronnie McKinnon	Belgium	3 February 1971	0–3 (l)
John Greig	N. Ireland	18 May 1971	0–1 (l)
Derek Johnstone	Brazil	30 June 1973	0–1 (l)

❋ RANGERS BEAT 11 HONEST MEN 9–0 ❋

Ayr United, nicknamed "The Honest Men", suffered their worst ever league reverse when Rangers beat them 9–0 away.

❊ QUEEN'S PARK ❊

By the time Rangers had won their first Scottish FA Cup in 1894, Queen's Park had already won the trophy ten times: they reached the final of both the English and Scottish FA Cups in 1884, winning the Scottish Cup when Vale of Leven did not turn up for the final and narrowly missing out on what would have been a truly unique Double, when Blackburn Rovers beat them in the English FA Cup final. In 1887, the SFA decreed that clubs "belonging to this Association shall not be members of any other Association", thus ending the participation of Scottish clubs in the English FA Cup. Queen's Park had also reached the English FA Cup final in 1885, when they again lost to Blackburn Rovers.

❊ 1999 TREBLE WINNERS ❊

Manchester United were not the only team to win a Treble in 1999. Rod Wallace's goal was enough to see off Celtic and secure the 1999 Scottish FA Cup for Rangers and hand manager Dick Advocaat the domestic Treble in his first season at Ibrox[1]. In typical Old Firm fashion, the pace of the game was frenetic and, somehow, it remained goalless at half-time, although Paul Lambert had thundered a shot against the crossbar. However, Wallace's goal, although a somewhat scrappy one, sent the Rangers faithful into delirium on the Hampden Park terraces. Alan Stubbs' attempted block from Neil McCann's effort fell kindly to Wallace, who gratefully knocked the ball past Jonathan Gould.

❊ NONE OF THEM IN THE RUNNING ❊

In October 1997, when Walter Smith announced at the Rangers AGM that he was stepping down as the manager of Rangers at the end of the season, the club was linked with a plethora of names as his successor. Names such as Bobby Robson, Terry Venables, Kenny Dalglish, Johan Cruyff, Richard Moller-Nielsen, Graeme Souness, Tommy Svensson, George Graham, Craig Brown and Sven-Goran Eriksson were all bandied about. Dutchman Dick Advocaat ultimately took over the reins at Ibrox.

---

[1] *Lorenzo Amoruso became only the sixth Rangers captain in the club's history to lead his side to the Treble. Late in the game, Amoruso bravely threw himself in front of a goal-bound effort from Lambert, but despite cries of "Penalty!" from the Celtic fans, who claimed that the Italian had used his hand, referee Hugh Dallas was having none of it and waved play on.*

✳ ALAN MORTON ✳

The esteem in which Alan Lauder Morton is held by everyone at Glasgow Rangers Football Club is self-evident from the portrait of the player affectionately nicknamed "The Wee Blue Devil" that stands at the top of the marble staircase in the main stand at Ibrox.

Alan began his career at Queen's Park but it wasn't long before a player who only stood 5ft 4in tall came to the attention of the Rangers manager, Bill Struth. In 1920, Morton joined Rangers. An unbelievably quick winger with tree trunk-like thighs who possessed excellent close ball control, the Wee Blue Devil tortured defences all across Scotland and on the international stage. He earned his infamous nickname following a mesmeric performance for Scotland against England on 31 March 1928 when Scotland annihilated England 5–1 at Wembley Stadium. Throughout the game Morton tortured the England full-backs, Frederick Goodall and Harry Jones, providing cross after cross for the Scottish attack. Indeed he provided three superb crosses from which Alex Jackson bagged a hat-trick. Morton and the Scottish side that played that day became heroes and are still fondly remembered as "The Wembley Wizards".

Alan made his international debut for Scotland as a Queen's Park player on 26 February 1920 in a 1–1 draw with Wales. He was one of seven players capped for the first time in the game, including Rangers' Thomas Cairns who scored Scotland's equalizer. Morton's first goal for his country came in his second appearance when Scotland beat Ireland 3–0 at Parkhead on 13 March 1920. By the time he won his third cap, Morton was a Rangers player and made 29 international appearances for his country during his Ibrox career. On 8 May 1932, Alan played his 31st and final game for Scotland in their 3–1 win over France in the Stade Olympique Colombes in Paris.

Morton's trademark move was his unerring ability to accurately turn a defender on the bye-line and then float in a pinpoint cross for a colleague to nod in at the far post. Alan Morton spent 13 years at Ibrox and enjoyed tremendous success. In total he played 495 times for Rangers, scoring 105 goals and setting up hundreds of others for his team-mates during his 13-year tenure. Morton won nine Scottish First Division Championship winners' medals and collected three Scottish Cup-winners' medals with the light blues. The name of Alan Morton will last forever in the history of Glasgow Rangers Football Club, a tremendous servant to both club and country.

Did You Know That?
Alan Morton was the first player that Bill Struth signed for Rangers.

✳ STRACHAN'S OLD FIRM BLUES ✳

Celtic's Neil Lennon and Alan Thompson were both sent off by referee Stuart Dougal during Celtic's 1–3 loss to Rangers at Ibrox on 20 August 2005 in what was Celtic manager Gordon Strachan's first Old Firm derby game.

✳ THIRD LANARK SNATCH MAJOR HONOURS ✳

In the 1903–04[†] season, Rangers and Celtic contested the Scottish FA Cup final at Hampden Park. The final had returned to its spiritual home after the four previous ones had been held at Ibrox Park (twice) and Celtic Park (twice). Celtic won the game 3–2 to claim their fourth cup success, thereby equalling the four cups won by Rangers – although both clubs still trailed Queen's Park by six cup wins. However, it was Third Lanark who dominated the season, winning the Scottish championship for the first and only time in the club's history.

✳ OTHER CLUB HONOURS ✳

Emergency War League – 1940 (1)
Southern League – 1941, 1942, 1943, 1944, 1945, 1946 (6)
Dryborough Cup – 1979 (1)
Tennents' Sixes – 1984, 1989 (2)
Milk Cup – *(Premier Competition)* 1984, 1992.
　　　　　　(Junior Competition) 1985 (3)
Glasgow Merchants and Charity Cup – 1878–79, 1896–97, 1899–1900, 1903–04, 1905–06, 1906–07, 1908–09, 1910–11, 1918–19, 1921–22, 1922–23, 1924–25, 1927–28, 1928–29, 1929–30, 1930–31, 1931–32, 1932–33, 1933–34, 1938–39, 1939–40, 1940–41, 1941–42, 1943–44, 1944–45, 1945–46, 1946–47, 1947–48, 1950–51, 1954–55, 1956–57, 1959–60 (32)
Glasgow Cup – 1893, 1894, 1897, 1898, 1900, 1901, 1902, 1911, 1912, 1913, 1914, 1918, 1919, 1922, 1923, 1924, 1925, 1930, 1932, 1933, 1934, 1936, 1937, 1938, 1940, 1942, 1943, 1944, 1945, 1948, 1950, 1954, 1957, 1958, 1960, 1969, 1971, 1975*, 1976, 1979, 1983, 1985, 1986, 1987 (44) *1975 trophy shared with Celtic after a 2–2 draw*
Glasgow League – 1895–96, 1897–98 (2)

[†]*In the 1903–04 season, the International Board ruled that goals could be scored direct from free-kicks that had been awarded for intentional fouls. Referees were also offered the discretion to play advantage following a foul or an offence.*

❊ SCOTTISH FOOTBALL'S HALL OF FAME ❊

John Cairney's superb book, *A Scottish Football Hall of Fame*, lists Scotland's top 100 internationals. Celtic lead the way with 23 entries, closely followed by Rangers with 22. Here are the Rangers players listed (along with their top-100 placing):

Jack Drummond (12)
Neilly Gibson (14)
Nicol Smith (17)
John Robertson (18)
Alec Smith (19)
Bob Hamilton (20)
Alan Morton (31)
Andy Cunningham (33)
Davie Meiklejohn (35)
Bob McPhail (40)
Jimmy Simpson (46)

Jerry Dawson (47)
Willie Waddell (53)
Willie Woodburn (54)
George Young (55)
Eric Caldow (70)
Jim Baxter (76)
Willie Henderson (78)
John Greig (79)
Graeme Souness (92)
Davie Cooper (95)
Ally McCoist (100)

❊ OLD FIRM PRETTY IN PINK ❊

On 7 April 1900, Scotland beat England 4–1 at Celtic Park in the Home Championship, earning Scotland the title of British champions for the eighth time outright plus two shared championships with England. Lord Rosebery persuaded the Scottish Football Association to allow the Scotland team to wear his horseracing colours of pink and primrose. Rangers had five players in the Scotland team, which lined up as follows: Henry George Rennie (Heart of Midlothian), Nicol Smith (Rangers), John Drummond (Rangers), Neil Gibson (Rangers), Alexander Galloway Raisbeck (Liverpool), John Tait Robertson (captain, Rangers), John Bell (Celtic), Robert Walker (Heart of Midlothian), Robert Smyth McColl (Queen's Park), John Campbell (Celtic), Alexander Smith (Rangers).

❊ THERE'S ONLY ONE JOHN PARROTT ❊

On the final day of the 2000–01 season, Ally McCoist played his last professional football game. Ally was in the Kilmarnock side that took on Celtic at Rugby Park and received a standing ovation from the Killie faithful after having helped Kilmarnock to fourth place in the Scottish Premier League. The Celtic fans, on the other hand, sang "There's Only One John Parrott" as Ally left the field, in reference to Ally's opposing team captain on the BBC show, *A Question of Sport*.

❊ UP FOR THE CUP (13) ❊

In the 2002–03 season, Rangers won the Scottish League Cup with a fine 2–1 win over Celtic in the final and edged past Celtic, on goal difference, to clinch the Scottish Premier League. In the Scottish Cup, Rangers disposed of Arbroath 3–0 away in the third round and then beat Ayr United 1–0 away in the fourth round. In the quarter-finals, they disposed of Dunfermline Athletic 3–0 in a replay at Ibrox – after drawing the first game 1–1 – and then narrowly squeezed past Motherwell, 4–3, in the semi-finals. A goal from Lorenzo Amoruso in the final was enough to secure them the Treble in Alex McLeish's first full season in charge of the club.

SCOTTISH FA CUP FINAL
31 MAY 2003, HAMPDEN PARK, GLASGOW
Rangers (0) 1   v.   Dundee (0) 0
(Amoruso)

Att. 47,136

Rangers: Stefan Klos, Fernando Ricksen, Arthur Numan, Lorenzo Amoruso, Craig Moore, Barry Ferguson, Shota Arverladze, Bob Malcolm, Ronald de Boer, Michael Mols, Neil McCann.
Subs: Allan McGregor, Steven MacLean, Steven Thompson, Maurice Ross, Kevin Muscat.

Did You Know That?
In the Old Firm game at Ibrox on 7 December 2002, Celtic's Chris Sutton stunned the home fans with a goal after just 18 seconds, the fastest goal ever scored in an Old Firm game. However, Rangers rallied to win 3–2 with goals from Moore, De Boer and Mols.

❊ 'GERS FRIGHTENED BY SPIDERS ❊

During the 1907–08 season, Queen's Park[†], nicknamed "The Spiders", beat Rangers 3–1 at Hampden Park and drew 1–1 at Ibrox Park in the Scottish First Division.

[†]*Queen's Park innovated the use of crossbars, free-kicks and half-time into the modern game. The first official international match between Scotland and England, played in Glasgow on 30 November 1872, was organized by Queen's Park and played under the club's rules. The Scotland team that drew 0–0 with the Auld Enemy consisted entirely of Queen's Park players, who wore their dark blue club jerseys. The Scottish national team adopted these colours shortly afterwards and as a result the club changed its home colours to black and white hoops in 1873, which is why the club are also known as "The Hoops".*

❋ RANGERS' FIRST CUP FINAL GOAL ❋

Rangers' first ever goal in the Scottish Cup final was not scored by a Rangers player; MacDougall of Vale of Leven scored an own goal in the 1–1 draw on 17 March 1877. Rangers drew the replay 1–1 (scorer: Dunlop) on 7 April 1877 and went on to lose the second replay 3–2 on 13 April 1877 (scorers: Campbell and W. McNeil). Watson from Rangers scored an own goal in the defeat.

❋ DEBT-RIDDEN CLUB BEAT RANGERS ❋

During the 1894–95 season, Partick Thistle's Glasgow Cup game against Dykebar had to be hastily arranged after their scheduled game against Pollokshaws was cancelled because Pollokshaws were under an SFA suspension. Partick Thistle won the re-arranged tie and progressed to the semi-finals – where they faced Rangers at Inchview. Everyone anticipated an easy win for Rangers and a bumper pay day – as Celtic awaited the winners in the final. However, in their previous 11 meetings at Inchview, Rangers had never beaten Thistle, with the home side winning eight of their previous 17 games against Rangers.

Wilkie scored an early goal to give Thistle the lead, while at the other end, Pat Smith saved six good chances from the Rangers forward line. In the second half, Rangers scored an equalizer, but it was controversially disallowed for handball. Partick held on for a win and what they presumed to be a place in the Glasgow Cup final. However, Rangers lodged an appeal with the Glasgow FA, pointing out that "The Jags'" goalkeeper, Pat Smith, had played in a five-a-side competition for his former club, Duntocher Harp, after he had signed for Thistle. The Glasgow FA upheld the protest from Rangers and ordered a replay. The game was replayed at Inchview and this time Rangers won 5–3 to record their first ever victory over Thistle at the ground.

❋ RANGERS WIN 70-MINUTE GAME ❋

At the beginning of the 1895–96 season, Rangers entertained Partick Thistle[†] at Ibrox Park in a benefit match for J. Black. Rangers won a 70-minute game 5–1.

[†]Prior to the first game against Rangers, it was revealed that Thistle had a debt of £16 10 shillings carried over from the previous season. However, estimates put Partick's net income from the two games at £180, thus pleasing the club's bankers by cancelling out the debt.

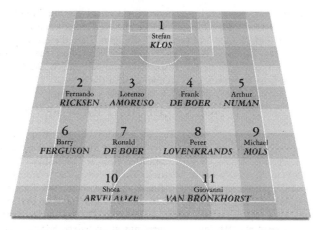

✹ RANGERS XI OF THE 2000s ✹

1
Stefan
KLOS

2
Fernando
RICKSEN

3
Lorenzo
AMORUSO

4
Frank
DE BOER

5
Arthur
NUMAN

6
Barry
FERGUSON

7
Ronald
DE BOER

8
Peter
LOVENKRANDS

9
Michael
MOLS

10
Shota
ARVELADZE

11
Giovanni
VAN BRONKHORST

Reserves
Ronald *WATTEROUS* • Henning *BERG* • Chris *BURKE*
Dado *PRSO* • Claudio *CANNIGIA*
Manager
Alex *McLEISH*

Did You Know That?
On 8 March 2006, Rangers narrowly missed out on becoming the first Scottish club to reach the quarter-final stages of the Champions League when they drew 1–1 away to Villareal. Rangers went out of the competition on the away-goals rule after drawing the first leg 2–2.

✹ DARK BLUES' RECORD HOME ATTENDANCE ✹

In 1953, the record home attendance for Dens Park was set when Rangers played Dundee there in front of 43,024 fans. Dundee are nicknamed "The Dark Blues".

✹ BUD ✹

Willie Johnston used to wear a full-length fur coat when he went out for the night in Glasgow and, as a result, he was nicknamed "Bud", because the only other man who did that was the comedian, Bud Flanagan, of Flanagan and Allen.

❋ THE DAVIE COOPER CUP FINAL ❋

The Scottish Football League marked the tenth anniversary of the death of Davie Cooper by featuring the former Scotland winger's image on the tickets for the 2005 League Cup final between Rangers and Motherwell, two of the three clubs that Cooper had served during his illustrious career. The final, won by Rangers, took place at Hampden Park on 20 March, three days before the date of his tragic death in 1995 after he had succumbed to a brain haemorrhage at the age of 39. SFL secretary Peter Donald said: "It is an acknowledgement of his involvement with both clubs, and it was felt that featuring Davie on every match ticket for the final would provide both sets of fans with an appropriate memento. It is a celebration of the pleasure he brought to both clubs and to Scottish football in general." In addition, CIS, the tournament sponsor, donated 25 pence from every final programme sold at Hampden to help establish "The Davie Cooper Centre", a custom-built facility for children with special needs in Glasgow. Terry Butcher, the Motherwell manager, and a former team-mate of Davie's both at Rangers and Motherwell, said: "I think it's a really nice touch by the League and a lovely way to remember his influence on both clubs. People will be able to look back at the tickets in years to come and remember it as the Davie Cooper final. It's hard to believe that it's ten years since he was taken from us. It still feels like such a travesty to me, because not only was he a terrific man, but he would also have put so much back into football as either a coach or manager."

❋ RECORD WINNING MARGIN ❋

In the 1999–2000 season, Rangers claimed their 49th Scottish championship in style, winning the title by a record 21-point margin over Celtic.

❋ ORANGE BLUES ❋

Dick Advocaat signed Ronald de Boer for Rangers on 31 August 2000 from Barcelona. He joined fellow Dutch internationals Arthur Numan, Giovanni van Bronckhorst, Michael Mols, Bert Konterman and Fernando Ricksen. Ronald de Boer spent four seasons at Ibrox before teaming up with his twin brother, Frank, at the Qatar club, Al-Rayyan. He played 91 league games for Rangers and scored 32 league goals. He also won 67 caps for Holland and scored 13 international goals. Frank, too, briefly played for Rangers in 2004.

❋ FREE PLAYER ❋

In the summer of 1998, Rod Wallace signed for Rangers for free under the Bosman ruling – and what a bargain he proved to be for Rangers. Wallace scored on his Rangers debut and tortured defences with his speed and vicious body swerves on the wing. He found the net 27 times in 51 outings during his first season at Ibrox – a remarkable return from a winger. Rod left Ibrox in 2001.

❋ EIGHT FROM EIGHT ❋

In the 2004–05 season, Rangers were put out of the Scottish Cup by Celtic, losing 2–1 in the third round at Celtic Park. It was Rangers' eighth successive away draw in the competition and their seventh successive away draw in the competition to Celtic since the 1963–64 season.

❋ THE BIG MAN ❋

Rangers signed Lorenzo Amoruso[1] from Fiorentina during the 1997–98 season and immediately threw him in at the deep end: he made his competitive debut in an Old Firm derby and it was an enjoyable one as, on 5 April 1998, Rangers beat Celtic 2–1 in their Scottish Cup semi-final encounter. The game was played at the "neutral" Celtic Park, as Hampden Park was still being redeveloped at the time. Amoruso went on to make 148 league appearances for Rangers, scoring 13 times, and will always hold a special place in the hearts of Rangers fans as he was a part of two Treble winning teams. On 14 July 2003, he signed for Blackburn Rovers in a deal worth £1.4 million.

❋ GAZZA PAYS PENALTY FOR BUST-UP ❋

Paul Gascoigne missed all of Rangers' matches in December 1997 when he was banned for five games by the SFA. Gazza, who was sent off for violent conduct in the Old Firm match at Celtic Park on 19 November 1997, had already chalked up nine disciplinary points for accumulated bookings. His sending-off against Celtic cost him another 12 points, taking his total to 21 and over the disciplinary threshold. The game ended in a 1–1 draw.

---

[1] Lorenzo began his professional career with his hometown club Bari and then had spells with Mantova, Pescavo and Fiorentina.

❊ WILLIE WADDELL ❊

William Waddell was born in Forth, Lanarkshire, on 7 March 1921. A right-winger, he possessed the strength and physical make-up of a strong centre-forward. Waddell joined Rangers from school and aged 15 he was farmed out to Strathclyde to gain experience. In 1938, aged 17, he made his debut for the club in the annual encounter with Arsenal, a game in which he scored the only goal. A week later he made his league debut for Rangers in a 4–1 win over Ayr.

In addition to his power, Waddell possessed excellent close ball control skills and was lightning quick. Having made ten unofficial appearances for Scotland during the Second World War, Waddell won his first official international cap for Scotland on 19 October 1946 in a 3–1 win over Wales at the Racecourse Ground, Wrexham, in a British Home International Championship game. Waddell scored Scotland's first goal from the penalty spot. Waddell went on to make a further 16 appearances for Scotland, making 27 appearances in total for his country.

During the Second World War, Waddell played for Rangers in area leagues and helped them to all seven league titles competed for during this time, and remarkably he also helped Rangers win 25 of the 34 wartime competitions they entered. With Rangers, his only club as a player, Waddell won four Scottish First Division Championship winners' medals and two Scottish Cup-winners' medals. However, he missed out on the inaugural Scottish League Cup final in 1947 when Rangers beat Aberdeen 4–0. Waddell played a total of 558 matches for Rangers, scoring 143 goals from 1938 to 1956.

In 1956, he was appointed the manager of Kilmarnock and led them to their only Scottish First Division League Championship in 1964–65. Following his success at Kilmarnock, Waddell returned to Ibrox in 1969 and became manager. In 1970, Waddell brough a six-year trophyless run to an end when Rangers won the Scottish League Cup. However, Waddell's greatest achievement came in 1972 when he guided Rangers to European Cup-Winners' Cup glory, beating Dynamo Moscow 3–2 in the final at Camp Nou, Barcelona. Following their European triumph, Waddell handed the manager's job over to Jock Wallace. He went on to serve the club as managing director, general manager and vice-chairman until his death in 1992. Following the Ibrox Disaster in 1971, when 66 fans lost their lives, Waddell set about ensuring such a fateful incident would never happen again and was the driving force behind the improvement of the stadium which today is one of only 12 stadia across Europe that have been awarded a five-star UEFA rating.

❋ WIT AND WISDOM OF THE BLUES (20) ❋

"What do I like about Rangers? I like winning."
Mark Hateley, after scoring a goal on his return to Rangers in 1997

❋ WASPS STUNG ❋

Rangers have only ever met Alloa Athletic[†] twice in the Scottish First Division. In the 1922–23 season, Rangers won all four points from the two fixtures, with 2–0 wins both at home and away.

❋ RANGERS' FIRST EUROPEAN ADVENTURE ❋

Rangers, the champions of Scotland at the time, entered European competition for the first time in 1956–57 and were knocked out in the first round by OGC Nice. Rangers won 2–1 at Ibrox, but lost by the same score in the Stade Municipal du Ray, Nice, in the away leg. The French champions won the play-off game 3–1, as the away-goals rule was not in operation at the time.

❋ YOUNG'S CONSECUTIVE CAPS RECORD ❋

George Young holds the Rangers record for the highest number of consecutive appearances for Scotland with 34. The sequence began on 10 April 1948 with a 2–0 home defeat by England and ended on 4 November 1953 with a 3–3 home draw against Wales.

❋ BIG AL'S 23 IN A ROW ❋

Future Rangers manager Alex McLeish made 23 consecutive appearances for Scotland between 28 May 1983 and 4 December 1985, while he was a player with Aberdeen.

❋ BLUES OUTDONE BY SOUTH AMERICANS ❋

Uruguay, two-time World Cup winners, beat Scotland 3–2 on 2 May 1962 in a World Cup warm-up friendly at Hampden Park in front of 67,181 fans. There were seven Old Firm players in Scotland's team that day, including their two goalscorers, Jim Baxter and Ralph Brand. But Uruguay went on to have a disappointing World Cup finals in 1962.

[†]*Alloa Athletic are nicknamed "The Wasps" because of their distinctive yellow-and-black striped shirts.*

❋ RANGERS IN FIRST PLACE ❋

Up to the end of the 2005–06 season, taking the three domestic trophies as a whole, Rangers top the success charts having won 106 trophies (51 league, 31 Scottish FA Cup and 24 Scottish League Cup). Celtic have won 86 (40, 33 and 13) with Aberdeen in third position on 16 trophies (four, seven and five).

❋ RECORD INTERNATIONAL CROWD ❋

On 17 April 1937, Scotland thrashed England 4–2 at Hampden Park in front of a record-breaking crowd of 149,547 spectators (official)[†]. Unofficially, it is estimated that as many as 159,547 spectators may have been in attendance, as it was reported that fans broke down the gates in their eagerness to watch the game. Rangers' Bob McPhail scored twice in the game alongside three of his Ibrox team-mates. The Scotland team to line up that day was as follows: James (Jerry) Dawson (Rangers), Andrew Anderson (Heart of Midlothian), Andrew Beattie (Preston North End), Alexander Massie (Aston Villa), James McMillan Simpson (captain, Rangers), George Clark Phillips Brown (Rangers), James Delaney (Celtic), Thomas Walker (Heart of Midlothian), Francis O'Donnell (Preston North End), Robert Low McPhail (Rangers), Douglas (Dally) Duncan (Derby County).

❋ OLD FIRM DOMINATE SCOTTISH CUP WINS ❋

The Old Firm have dominated the Scottish Cup, with Celtic leading the way on 33 wins to Rangers' 30. Queen's Park are in third place with ten triumphs, although their last win was way back in 1893. Next up are Aberdeen, with seven – all of which were achieved after the Second World War – and 2006 winners Hearts, also with seven.

❋ ALBION ROVERS DENY RANGERS ❋

After a drawn Scottish Cup semi-final and replay, Albion Rovers beat Rangers 2–0 at Celtic Park in the second replay in April 1920. It was Albion's first season in the league and, as there was only one Scottish League at the time, Rovers equalled Dumbarton's feat – in 1897 – of reaching the Scottish Cup final while sitting at the bottom of the league.

[†] *The attendance of 149,547 remains the largest crowd ever to have watched an international match in Europe.*

❉ RANGERS PLAYER BANNED FOR LIFE ❉

Between 1938 and 1954, Willie Woodburn[†], nicknamed "Wicked Willie", played 325 games for Rangers, scoring just one goal. During his Ibrox career, he won four league titles, four Scottish Cups and two League Cups (three Doubles and a Treble). He also won 24 caps for Scotland. Despite being noted for possessing a fiery temper, it was ten years into his Rangers career before he received his first yellow card. In August 1948, Woodburn was involved in a violent exchange with Motherwell's centre-forward Dave Mathie and was subsequently suspended by the SFA for 14 days. He remained "calm" for a further five years and then, on 7 March 1953, he took a swing at Billy McPhail of Clyde ... but missed. He was sent off and the SFA handed out a 21-day ban for his misdemeanour. Johnny Hubbard, Woodburn's South African team-mate at Ibrox, said: "I don't know what he would have got had he made contact." Then, on 28 August 1954, at Ibrox, Woodburn head-butted Stirling's young centre-forward Alec Paterson after he had been on the receiving end of a nasty challenge from Paterson. As a result of the incident, the SFA banned Willie from the game *sine die*, for life. Woodburn appealed the decision, but when the SFA finally lifted his ban on 23 April 1957, he was 38 years old and too old to play.

❉ DALLAS TAKES OVER OLD FIRM ❉

On 19 November 1995, Scottish referee Hugh Dallas[††] took charge of his first ever Old Firm derby match. The game was played at Ibrox Park and ended 3–3.

❉ GOUGH THE OLD FIRM PEACEMAKER ❉

Whenever Richard Gough captained Rangers in an Old Firm game refereed by Hugh Dallas, he would always approach the referee at the coin-toss and inform him that if any of the Rangers players stepped out of line, then Mr Dallas should come and see him to sort them out. Mr Dallas – who refereed several Old Firm clashes during his career – normally responded with: "Yes, but who do I speak to when you step out of line?"

[†]*Woodburn hated losing so much that he once threw a pair of football boots through a glass window at Hampden Park after Rangers had lost a Scottish Cup semi-final there.*
[††]*During the game, Dallas handed out nine yellow cards, disallowed a goal and watched as a fan ran across the pitch and jumped in behind the technical areas.*

✳ SCOTTISH LEAGUE CUP KINGS ✳

The Old Firm have dominated the Scottish League Cup since its inception in 1947 with Rangers clearly leading the way with 24 wins to Celtic's 13. Aberdeen lie in third place with five triumphs.

✳ CLUB RECORD START – 18 OUT OF 18 ✳

Between 20 August 1898 and 7 January 1899, Rangers won their opening 18 league games of the season. They went on to claim their first championship at the end of the season.

✳ McLEISH DRAWS RECORD BLANK ✳

Rangers boss Alex McLeish holds the record for having made the most appearances (77) for Scotland without ever scoring a goal for his country.

✳ SCORING INTERNATIONAL DEBUTANTS ✳

Peter Campbell (two goals) was the first Rangers player to score on his debut for Scotland. He found the net in Scotland's 9–0 win over Wales on 23 March 1878. Rangers' James Watson also scored on his debut in the same game. Up until the end of the 2004–05 season, 18 Rangers players have equalled the feat – the highest number of players from any club.

✳ GREIG'S VICTORY GOAL ✳

Rangers' John Greig scored the only goal of the game to give Scotland a 1–0 win over Italy at Hampden Park on 9 November 1965 in a World Cup qualifying game. Greig's fellow Rangers teammates in the victorious Scotland side included Willie Henderson, Ronnie McKinnon and Davie Provan.

✳ ROBERT DUVALL MANAGES ALLY McCOIST ✳

In the movie *A Shot at Glory*, the famous American actor Robert Duvall plays the part of the manager of Kilnockie Knockies, a fictional second-tier Scottish football club, who is forced to hire the services of journeyman footballer, Ally McCoist, to improve the fortunes of the team and prevent it from being moved away from the fiercely loyal town it has played in for a century.

❋ BIBLIOGRAPHY & REFERENCES ❋

WEBSITES

www.absoluteastronomy.com ❖ www.answers.com
www.answers.com ❖ www.ayeready.com
www.bbc.co.uk ❖ www.comeonthehoops.com
www.cowdenbeath.net ❖ www.eleven-a-side.com
www.englandfanzine.co.uk ❖ www.englandfc.com
www.englandfootballonline.com ❖ www.eveningtimes.co.uk
www.eveningtimes.co.uk ❖ www.forfarathletic-mad.co.uk
www.geocities.com ❖ www.glasgowguide.co.uk
www.goalkeepersaredifferent.com ❖ www.guardian.co.uk
www.londonhearts.com ❖ www.napit.co.uk
www.nozdrul.plus.com ❖ www.onetel.net.uk
www.prideofanglia.com ❖ www.psychcentral.com
www.ptearlyyears.net ❖ www.rsssf.com
www.scotland-guide.co.uk ❖ www.scottishleague.net
www.soccerbase.com/teams.sd ❖ www.soccerfansnetwork.com
www.sport.scotsman.com ❖ www.sportcartoons.co.uk
www.sporting-heroes.net ❖ www.sundaymirror.co.uk
www.thisisthenortheast.co.uk ❖ www.uk.geocities.com
www.upyarkilt.com ❖ www.wikipedia.org

BOOKS

- *The Little Book of Rangers* edited by Neil Cameron, Carlton Publishing Group, 2004
- *The Official Rangers Supporters' Book* by Graham Hunter, Carlton Publishing Group, 1997
- *Rangers* by Ian Morrison, Hamlyn Publishing Group Limited, 1988
- *The Daily Telegraph Football Chronicle* by Norman Barrett, Carlton Publishing Group, 2004
- *Rangers – The Complete Record* by Bob Ferrier and Robert McElroy, The Breedon Books Publishing Company Limited, 2005
- *A Record of Post-War Scottish League Players,* John Lister and *Scottish Football Historian* magazine